International Management Accounting in Japan

Current Status of Electronics Companies

Monden Institute of Management: Japanese Management and International Studies (ISSN: 1793-2874)

Editor-in-Chief: Yasuhiro Monden *(Mejiro University, Japan)*

Published

Vol. 1   Value-Based Management of the Rising Sun
edited by Yasuhiro Monden, Kanji Miyamoto, Kazuki Hamada, Gunyung Lee & Takayuki Asada

Vol. 2   Japanese Management Accounting Today
edited by Yasuhiro Monden, Masanobu Kosuga, Yoshiyuki Nagasaka, Shufuku Hiraoka & Noriko Hoshi

Vol. 3   Japanese Project Management:
KPM — Innovation, Development and Improvement
edited by Shigenobu Ohara & Takayuki Asada

Vol. 4   International Management Accounting in Japan:
Current Status of Electronics Companies
edited by Kanji Miyamoto

Monden Institute of Management
Japanese Management and International Studies – Vol. 4

International Management Accounting in Japan

Current Status of Electronics Companies

editor

Kanji Miyamoto

Osaka Gakuin University, Japan

 **World Scientific**

NEW JERSEY · LONDON · SINGAPORE · BEIJING · SHANGHAI · HONG KONG · TAIPEI · CHENNAI

Published by

World Scientific Publishing Co. Pte. Ltd.

5 Toh Tuck Link, Singapore 596224

USA office: 27 Warren Street, Suite 401-402, Hackensack, NJ 07601

UK office: 57 Shelton Street, Covent Garden, London WC2H 9HE

British Library Cataloguing-in-Publication Data
A catalogue record for this book is available from the British Library.

Monden Institute of Management: Japanese Management and International Studies — Vol. 4
INTERNATIONAL MANAGEMENT ACCOUNTING IN JAPAN:
Current Status of Electronics Companies

Copyright © 2008 by World Scientific Publishing Co. Pte. Ltd.

ISBN-13 978-981-277-956-4
ISBN-10 981-277-956-6

Typeset by Stallion Press
Email: enquiries@stallionpress.com

Printed in Singapore.

Monden Institute of Management

The Mission of the Institute and Editorial Information

For the purpose of making a contribution to the business and academic communities, Monden Institute of Management is committed to publishing the book series coherently entitled *Japanese Management and International Studies*, a kind of book-length journal with a referee system.

Focusing on Japan and Japan-related issues, the series is designed to inform the world about research outcomes of the new "Japanese-style management system" developed in Japan. It includes the Japanese version of management systems developed abroad. In addition, it publishes research by overseas scholars and concerning overseas systems that constitute significant points of comparison with the Japanese system.

Research topics included in this series are management of organization in a broad sense (including the business group) and the accounting that supports the organization. More specifically, topics include business strategy, organizational restructuring, corporate finance, M&A, environmental management, business models, operations management, managerial accounting,

v

financial accounting for organizational restructuring, manager performance evaluation, remuneration systems, and management of revenues and costs. The research approach is interdisciplinary, which includes case studies, theoretical studies, normative studies, and empirical studies.

Each volume contains the series title and a book title which reflects the volume's special theme.

Our institute's board of directors has established an editorial board of international standing. In each volume, guest editors who are experts on the volume's special theme will serve as the volume editors.

Editorial Board of
Japanese Management and International Studies

Kenneth A. Merchant, University of Southern California, USA
Yoshiteru Minagawa, Nagoya Gakuin University, Japan
Kanji Miyamoto, Osaka Gakuin University, Japan
Tengku Akbar Tengku Abdullah, Universiti Kebangsaan Malaysia, Malaysia
Jimmy Y.T. Tsay, National Taiwan University, Taiwan
Susumu Ueno, Konan University, Japan
Eri Yokota, Keio University, Japan
Walid Zaramdini, UAE University, United Arab Emirates

Preface

This book discusses the current status of International Management Accounting in Japan through the interviews with three major electronics companies in Japan and investigations into their evolving international business activities and their accompanying organizational structure, management, and management accounting (especially international management accounting).

This book consists of two parts. Part 1 describes the general concepts of international management accounting on the premise that the international management accounting system is established in conformity with corporate strategy, under which organizational structure and management are adopted in the pursuit of the organization's strategic objectives.

The first paper discusses the pattern of international organization structure on the premise that the international management accounting system is affected by changes to organizational structure and will change as the organization's structure changes. Thus, the organizational structure and the information system will change as companies transit from being domestic companies to multinational and global companies. Therefore, the change of organizational structure, and its accompanying change of responsibilities, requires an accompanying change in the information system (including management accounting system).

The second paper discusses the global or transnational strategies that involve the configuration, co-ordination, and integration of geographically dispersed business activities. In order to plan, implement, and control global strategy, strategic management and international management accounting systems have to be established and effective international management accounting information should be provided.

When the company adopts a global strategy, the company actually tries to achieve global scale economic efficiency, while simultaneously adapting to local market needs and learning capability. The company with a global strategy establishes an integral network connecting financial resource distribution and strategic business units. Here, it is essential for the international management accounting system to have good communications between the global headquarters and subsidiaries (and also between each subsidiary) so that relevant information is transmitted in timely fashion. As representative examples of this international management accounting information, three types of information — multicurrency accounting information, accounting information required for budget management in global companies, and accounting information using a composite currency as the measurement unit in global companies — are described.

In Part 2, the results of research and studies of the current international management accounting of three major electronics companies will be elaborated in order to clarify part of the current status of international management accounting in Japan. By tracing the history of the business expansion of the three companies in the electronics industry, transition of strategies and its accompanying transition of organizational structures, management, and details of international management accounting are faithfully described. In these studies, the manner in which the companies' present strategies were developed, conducted and managed is verified through interviews in order to find out the international management accounting of the three companies. Additionally, the characteristics of the international management accounting of the three companies are also clarified.

The third paper investigates the current status of the international management accounting practices of Matsushita Electric Industrial Co., Ltd. Matsushita Electric Industrial Co., Ltd. has been developed through performing management with the profit center approach, which was first introduced in Japan in 1932 by Mr. Konosuke Matsushita, the founder of Matsushita Electric Industrial Co., Ltd. It had already started overseas business activities before World War II and had successfully developed there to become a global company. This helped the company survive the difficult times that followed Japan's defeat in the war.

The fourth paper researches and studies the current status of international management accounting practices of Sharp Corporation which was established in 1912. Starting with the innovation of the mechanical pencil by Mr. Tokuji Hayakawa, the founder of Sharp Corporation, it has always created new market fields with products such as the first domestic radio, television, and the world's first calculator and LCD. Realization of Sharp's management principles ("Make Only-one Products") and its history of transition of strategies, management, and management accounting are reviewed through interviews which were carried out to find out the details of Sharp's current international management accounting.

The fifth paper investigates the current status of international management accounting at SANYO Electric Co., Ltd. The company name "SANYO" means three oceans — Pacific Ocean, Atlantic Ocean, and

Indian Ocean — and also implies the entire world is to be dealt with using the three pillars of human resources, technologies, and services. These pillars were thought of by Mr. Toshio Iue, the founder of the company, who had ambitious hopes to extend his business throughout the world. In 1949, two years after starting the business in 1947, overseas trade had already been started, and the company successfully increased its business. The history of transition of strategies, management, and management accounting here is reviewed, based on which interviews were carried out to clarify the details of current international management accounting.

The sixth paper compares and reviews the international management accountings of the three major electronics companies which appeared in papers 3, 4, and 5, in order to clarify the characteristics of each company's international management accounting.

Finally, the contents of the study results in this book have been added and modified by all expert committee members of International Management Accounting in the enterprise research study project of the Japanese Association of Management Accounting. The purpose of this book is to benefit people abroad who are establishing theories and practices for their international management accountings. In addition, I would like to express special thanks to the people of Matsushita Electric Industrial Co., Ltd., Sharp Corporation, and SANYO Electric Co., Ltd., who graciously agreed to be interviewed for this study. Also, I would like to express deep and sincere gratitude to Prof. Yoichi Kataoka, the committee chairman of the enterprise research study project of the Japanese Association of Management Accounting, who helped to carry out research activities for this book. Lastly, I would like to express special thanks to Prof. Yasuhiro Monden, the founder of Monden Institute of Management, who made it possible for me to publish this book as book series Vol. 4 of the institute.

Editor
Kanji Miyamoto
15 October 2007

Contents

Part 1

International Management
Accounting Concepts

Strategy and Organizational Structure of Global Companies

Kanji Miyamoto

Professor of Accounting, Faculty of Corporate Intelligence
Osaka Gakuin University

1 Management Accounting System of Global Companies

The management accounting system of global companies should be established in conformity with corporate strategy, under which organizational structure and management process are adopted in the pursuit of each company's strategic objectives.

Mueller *et al.* (1987) point out the following with respect to an accounting information system for multinational corporations (which can be generalized to global companies): "The designer of an accounting system for an MNC must be aware of (1) the organization's nature and purpose, (2) the organizational structure, (3) the degree of centralization/decentralization, (4) the size of the MNC, and (5) management's basic philosophy and attitude toward foreign operations."

Also, Arpan and Radebaugh (1981) give the same opinion as described above: "A firm doing business internationally must thoroughly investigate the decision to be made before making it. This process is more difficult than the similar process for a domestic operation because the variables, alternatives, and unknowns are more numerous. For international operations to be successful, particularly those of a multinational enterprise, considerable attention must be devoted to information system, organizational structure, and control. Each must be carefully designed in itself and in terms of each other to make sure they are suitable and mutually supportive."

However, management accounting is part of an organization's information system which provides all levels of managers in organizations with useful information for corporate strategy and its management. It is necessary in the study of the management accounting of global companies

3

to understand the strategies of global companies, under which organizational structure and management are adopted in the pursuit of its strategic objectives.

This paper discusses the pattern of international organization structure on the premise that the international management system is affected by changes to organizational structure and will change as the organization's structure changes. Thus, the organizational structure and the information system will change as companies transit from being domestic companies to multinational and global companies. Therefore, the change of organizational structure, and its accompanying change of responsibilities, requires an accompanying change in the information system (including management accounting system).

It is necessary to define the terms "globalization" and "global business" used in this paper. The term "global" was first used in Levitt's (1983) article which implied a homogenized global market in terms of consumer needs and preferences. Yet the global refers to more than markets and is used to indicate global industry, global strategy, and global management. A global market refers to one which has broadly similar consumer needs and product preferences. A global industry is one which is a global configuration of value-adding activities within an industry. A global strategy which is used by Bartlett and Ghoshal (1989) as the term "transnational strategy" is one which develops global competitiveness, multinational flexibility, and worldwide learning capability simultaneously.

Chandler (1962) pointed out that structure follows strategy. The appropriate structure is to make strategy and its management work better. As companies transit from being domestic companies to international companies, they must cope with geographically dispersed operations, diverse social, cultural, political, legal, economic environments, and divergent trends in different countries. A domestic company does not have these challenges and so its organization structure is not appropriate for an international company. An appropriate organizational structure for an international company depends on its strategy to cope with increased global pressures.

As a result, according to Channon and Jalland (1979), "There is no one optimal organization form which should be adopted by the MNC. Rather the structure should be consistent with strategy in so far as this is possible. Moreover, since strategy itself tends to change over time so might organization structure expect to undergo modifications."

2 International Business Activities of Domestic Companies

At first, international operations of domestic companies begin with export sales to other countries. If such companies are organized along functional lines, export sales management is established along with domestic sales management in the sales department. On the other hand, if diversified domestically, the export sales division is established along with domestic product divisions and exports management tends to be centralized in order to be served by foreign sales specialists while domestic sales are serviced by sales managers of each domestic product division. It is not economical for each domestic product division to have an export specialist. The export sales division is also given responsibility for licensing and is treated as a profit center as well as production divisions.

An export sales division, however, suffer from two weakness. First, the export sales division is dependent on domestic divisions for both products and technology. Since the later concentrate their attention on domestic markets and limit their interest for foreign markets, they do not allow responsiveness to foreign markets based on sensitivity to their needs. Second, an export sales division functions effectively to further foreign market expansion through subcontracting and foreign direct investments because of the lack of experience in managing foreign operations.

As the companies' exports increase, each importing country's government begins to encourage local production by imposing restrictions such as tariffs and quotas. The exporting company establishes a production subsidiary inside the foreign market in order to protect its market share. The management of the foreign subsidiaries is given unlimited powers of decision and action as the parent company does not have sufficient international experience to manage the foreign operations. The foreign subsidiaries report directly to the chief or other top executive of the parent company. When the international operations change from export sales to a mix of export sales, licensing, and oversea production, the export sales division is not able to handle the management of the international operations efficiently.

3 International Division Structure

The parent company does not intervene in the operations of foreign subsidiaries as far as they earn profits and remit dividends. Therefore, the management of foreign subsidiaries is independent. But when foreign sales and manufacturing operations increase, the need for coordination between such operations and domestic product divisions becomes much greater. Moreover, there is a growing need for decisions regarding such opportunities as licensing, joint ventures, and foreign direct investments. As a result, the export sales division is developed into an international division in order to consolidate all the foreign operations of the company. According to Davis (1976), "When a corporation has four or more foreign manufacturing operations, it is likely to place them all into an international division, reporting to a single executive".

The international division is usually subdivided by geography and manages exports, licensing, subcontracting, foreign branches, and foreign subsidiaries. The head of the international division is generally delegated total authority and responsibility for the international operations from a senior executive at corporate headquarters. The international division is a profit center as well as domestic product divisions and makes up policy and strategies planning for international operations. A representative organization diagram for a company using an international division structure is shown in Figure 1.

There are several advantages with the international division structure. First, it coordinates all the international operations so as to raise the level of performance above that where foreign subsidiaries are autonomous. Second,

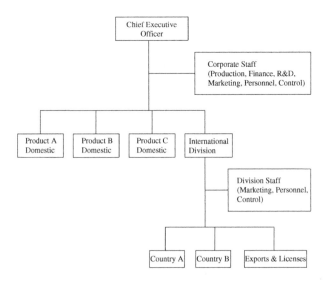

Fig. 1   International division structure

foreign operations are generally more complex than domestic operations. The presence of an international division forces managers to develop expertise in foreign operations. Third, since the international division is given generally total responsible for profits and losses of the foreign operations, its managers make top management cognizant of the results of decisions on international operations and the best overall corporate strategy for international profits.

There are, however, several disadvantages with the international division structure. First, the international division structure is the separation of domestic product divisions' managers from its international division's counterparts, which may turn out to be a drawback as the company will expand international operations. Second, as the international division centralizes many decisions of foreign operations, the competitive position of the foreign subsidiaries may be reduced by the time lag in securing decision from it. Third, because the international division does not have its own product development and research and development experts, it relies upon support from the domestic product divisions. But, as the domestic product divisions are evaluated solely by their domestic performance, they frequently become reluctant to supply what the international division needs. The continued foreign expansion of the company through foreign direct investments brings about the inherent conflict between the domestic product divisions and the international division. For example, capital budgeting and transfer pricing are substantial issues. This has led most companies to replace their international divisions with global structures to realize gains by coordinating and integrating operations on a worldwide scale by taking advantage of economies of scale.

4 Global Organizational Structures

In many industries, competition is on a global basis, with the result that companies must be responsible for the worldwide operations and use global structures. Global structures may be organized on functional, product, or geographical lines of responsibilities.

4.1 *The global functional structure*

The functional structure has been the form most often used by European companies. The global functional organization is organized by functions such as production, marketing, finance, research and development, and other functions. The heads of these functions have worldwide line responsibility for operations and management.

The global functional organization has the advantage of tight control over specific functions worldwide. It allows a relatively small group of officers to bring out competitive strengths in each function. The functional structure works rather well when companies remain comparatively small and have a few lines of products. However, this type of structure has some serious weaknesses. Coordination of functions is difficult, as this structure separates, for example, marketing from manufacturing. Subsidiaries normally have to report to several different persons at headquarters, resulting in tremendous duplication of effort. Finally, the structure is unsuitable for multi-product or geographically dispersed organization as each function may need its own product or regional specialists. As a consequence of such weaknesses, many companies organize their organization structures on product or geographical lines of responsibilities.

4.2   *The global geographic structure*

The geographic structure organizes the company on the basis of the geographical areas where it operates. Each area division has both product line and functional responsibility for all operations within its area, and corporate headquarters retains responsibility for worldwide strategy. A representative organization diagram for a company using a global geographic structure is shown in Figure 2.

The geographic structure is highly suited for mature businesses with narrow product lines but with geographically dispersed operations, because their growth potential is greater in abroad than in the domestic market where the products are at later stages in their life cycles. This structure also works well where the product is highly standardized, but techniques for penetrating markets differ. Therefore, it is essential for area managers to possess intimate knowledge of local conditions, constraints, and preferences. Worldwide standardization and area variegation may be incompatible. However, Davis (1976) pointed out that the major advantage of a global geographic structure was its ability to differentiate regional and local markets and determine variations in each appropriate market mix.

A geographic structure develops control systems that each local subsidiary is evaluated by the contribution toward the area division and the subsidiary managers need to be motivated to act in the best interests of the area division.

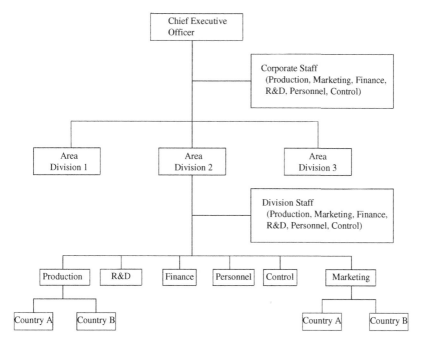

Fig. 2   Global geographic structure

A geographic structure usually requires the duplication of functional and product specialists at each area headquarters. This may create high organizational costs. This structure also may result in necessary information not reaching corporate headquarters because of the area managers' focus on area performance. Company's worldwide interest may therefore be opposed.

The structure also insulates one geographic unit from another, which may make it difficult to transfer new technologies, new product ideas, and production techniques across markets. When the company has a diverse product range, the geographic structure may become inappropriate.

4.3   *The global product structure*

The product structure is adopted by companies with multiple product lines. Every product comprises a division that is given worldwide responsibility for its design, production, and marketing. Consequently, each of the product division has its own functional, environmental, sales, and manufacturing responsibilities and functions as a profit center. Corporate headquarters

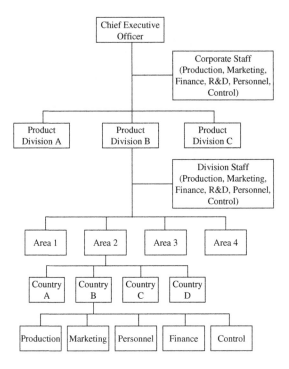

Fig. 3   Global product structure

sets overall goals and strategies for the company. These corporate guidelines provide both the protection and the constrains under which each product division is expected to formulate divisional plans by having its own functional staff. Such a structure is shown in Figure 3.

The global product structure works best when a company's product line is highly diversified, when the product divisions seldom use common marketing tools, channels or promotion, when a high level of technological capability is required, and when there is significant need to globally integrate production, marketing, and research related to the product.

The major advantage of the global product structure is the ease of flow of technology and product knowledge from the divisional level to the foreign subsidiaries. It is also advantageous when local labor cost and skill level, tariff and tax regulations, shipping costs, or other considerations facilitates the coordination and integration of production in different countries in order to produce the highest quality at the lowest cost.

The main weakness of a global product division is the duplication of facilities and staff groups that each division requires to support its own operations. Another is that worldwide responsibility is assigned to managers with particular product expertise but whose experience has been largely domestic. These managers have limited knowledge of geographic markets. Thus, the emphasis of the division may be on the domestic market.

A similar weakness is that the lack of experience and capability for dealing with international operations may create difficulties in assessing environmental conditions in foreign markets. Another weakness of the product structure is the difficulty of coordination and integration of the subsidiaries' activities in any given area.

4.4 *The global mixed structure*

A mixed structure combines two or more organizational dimensions simultaneously in order to make the most of the advantages of each global structure and to minimize the weaknesses of one.

Companies with a global geographic structure coordinate all product lines within each area, but at the expense of coordination between geographic areas for any one product line. For example, when they embark on placing a new product line in the market, each area division may not make discrimination in sales of the new product line as the line is generally small when considered a proportion of the whole within its division. Thus, they introduce a means to manage the new product line from a worldwide point of view as distinguished from geographical area management.

According to Davis (1976), companies with a global geographic structure introduce global product line management into their organization design, facing following reasons and conditions:

- sharp difference in marketing or production and supply;
- little or no interdependence between the main line and the new one;
- currently small, but potentially large, growth of the separated product; and
- to avoid rivalry and hostility among managers in the different products.

Companies with a global product structure have the opposite problem to companies with a global geographic structure. The global product structure satisfies the need to maximize technological linkages among the plants in each business unit which is diversified by each product line in the world.

This has, however, the weakness which is not able to coordinate subsidiaries' activities in each area. To cope with problems of coordinating this parallel management, companies must introduce geographic management in their existing product structure.

According to Davis (1976), companies with global product structure need to coordinate their operations in each area when

- they have at least two significant but organizationally independent business units there;
- there are economies to be gained from pooled information;
- there are benefits derivable from a more unified corporate identity;
- there is a discernible need for assessing and coordinating corporate programs and their implementation.

Global companies that are organized along product lines may subsequently have regional groupings or companies with a global geographic structure may have subsequent product groupings. However, coordination and simplicity across such structures are not kept for a long time because of complications and difficulty for managers to handle. The main weakness of the mixed structure is the duplication of various activities, which may be expensive.

4.5   *The global matrix structure*

Each of the four global structures discussed has advantages but also weaknesses. In order to preserve the advantages of each of these structures and to overcome their weaknesses, many global companies adopt global matrix structures which provide for a three-dimensional linking or overlapping of functions, areas, and products.

Under this three-dimensional structure, power and responsibility for global operations are shared among product divisions, geographic areas, and functional areas. A matrix structure is shown in Figure 4, which shows an arrangement whereby products in three product groups are sold in six geographic areas. Responsibility for a proposed expansion of sales of industrial equipment in the Far East is divided among an industrial equipment manager, a Far East regional manager, and finance and marketing managers at headquarters.

A foreign subsidiary manager may report simultaneously to an area manager as well as a product manager. A product manager shares with

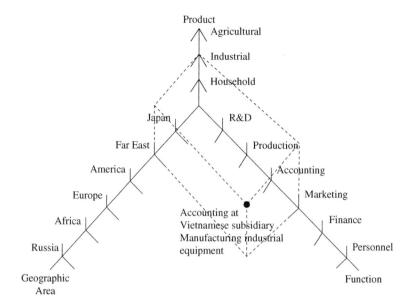

Fig. 4   Global matrix structure

an area manager responsibility for the profits of the foreign subsidiary. Managers must recognize the need to resolve issues and choices through frequent interchanges between the product and regional divisions.

In a matrix, the organization must adopt some fundamental changes in technical systems and management behavior and requires a commitment on the part of top management to the essential preparation required for it to be successful. It chooses two or more dimensions as the basis for grouping its operations.

The global matrix structure is one means of achieving global coordination and local responsiveness and is adopted if conditions such as the following exist:

- there is a diversification of products and areas;
- the opportunities are lost and significant problems created by favoring either the product or area dimension;
- two or more product, area, or functional divisions require the shared use of scarce resources;
- information, planning, and control system operate along the simultaneous consideration of functional, product, and area concerns;

- product and area demands require enriched information processing capacity because of uncertain, complex, and interdependent tasks.

An advantage of the matrix structure is that it forces the company to respond to all the important business factors, which can help to achieve both global coordination and national responsiveness simultaneously. In the matrix structure, reporting duplication with managers reporting to two or more bosses leads to more conflicts and confusion. Overlapping responsibilities have managers shirk their responsibilities. Also, the matrix design does take excessive time on decision-making process and increased administrative costs.

References

Arpan, J. S. and Radebaugh, L. H. (1981). *International Accounting and Multinational Enterprises*, Warren, Gorham & Lamont, Inc.

Bartlett, C. A. and Ghoshal, S. (1989). *Managing Across Borders: The Transnational Solution,* Harvard Business School Press.

Chandler, A. D. (1962). *Strategy and Structure: Chapters in the History of the American Industrial Enterprise*, MIT Press.

Channon, D. F. and Jalland, M. (1979). *Multinational Strategic Planning*, The Macmillan Press Ltd.

Davis, S. M. (1976). Trends in the organization of multinational corporations, *The Columbia Journal of World Business* 9(2), pp. 59–71.

Levitt, T. (1983). The globalization of market, *Harvard Business Review*, May/June, pp. 92–102.

Mueller, G. G., Gernon, H. and Meek, G. (1987). *Accounting: An International Perspective*, 2nd ed., Irwin.

Strategy and International Management Accounting of Global Companies

Kanji Miyamoto

Professor of Accounting, Faculty of Corporate Intelligence
Osaka Gakuin University

1 Introduction

In the 1980s and 1990s, many electronics companies in Japan aimed at globalizing. Globalizing means not only spreading activities around the globe but also using globally coherent strategies. In the investigations of electronics companies in Japan, it is necessary to define the concept of global strategy.

Bartlett and Ghoshal (1989) explored some provocative questions raised by the diverse experiences of nine worldwide companies and found three distinct models represented in these companies. These models were classified into multinational companies, classic global companies, and international companies. Bartlett and Ghoshal argued these companies as follows:

Multinational companies have developed a strategic posture and organizational capability that allow them to be very sensitive and responsive to differences in national environments around the world. In effect, these corporations manage a portfolio of multiple national entities. These corporations allow their overseas companies to operate quite independently. Classic global companies have developed international operations that are much more driven by the need for global efficiency, and much more centralized in their strategic and operational decisions. These companies treat the world market as an integrated whole. To these companies the global operating environment and worldwide consumer demand are the dominant units of analysis, not the nation–state or the local market. Products and strategies are developed to exploit an integrated unitary world market. International companies transfer and adapt the parent company's knowledge or expertise to foreign markets. The parent retains considerable influence and control, but less than in the classic global company; national units can adapt products and ideas coming from the center, but have less independence and autonomy than multinational subsidiaries.

According to the research of Bartlett and Ghoshal (1989), by the mid-1980s, the forces of global integration, local differentiation, and worldwide innovation had all become strong and compelling, and none could be ignored. To compete effectively, a company had to develop global competitiveness, multinational flexibility, and worldwide learning capability simultaneously.

2   Transnational Strategy

When managers in many worldwide companies are confronted with increasing complexity, diversity, and change, they look for ways to restructure. In theory, global matrix structure should work in this case. Namely, the matrix structure forces the company to respond to all important business factors, which can help it achieve both global coordination and national responsiveness simultaneously. For most companies, however, the result was disappointing.

In order to respond to the complexity and volatility of strategics task facing the worldwide company, its managers must achieve global efficiency, national responsiveness, and the ability to move and create knowledge on a worldwide basis. They perceive that there are irreconcilable contractions among the three objectives and tend to focus on one of them. The company that overcomes these contractions is called the transnational one by Bartlett and Ghoshal (1989). Also, such a company is called one with total global strategy by Yip (1992).

The company with transnational strategy can disperse or locate its value-chain activities anywhere in the world where its costs are cheap and additional value for its products and services is created. According to Cullen and Parboteeah (2005), costs or quality advantages associated with a particular nation are called national comparative advantage. Comparative advantage refers to advantages of nations over other nations. Location advantages for each value-chain activity provide low cost and high quality.

To increase global competitiveness, transnational companies can take advantage of economies of scale, scope, and factor costs, along with the changes in exchange rates, regulations, tastes, relative prices, and technologies. Therefore, they must build the capability to be responsive as exchange rates, regulations, tastes, and other factors change. Also, they can make innovations arise in many different parts of the organization.

The transnational company centralizes some resources and capabilities and distributes others among its many national subsidiaries. Production plants may be centralized in a low-wage country. Some resources may be distributed, yet the company specializes among local facilities to avoid exclusive dependence on a single facility and to protect against various disruptions (e.g., exchange rate shifts).

Multinational companies distributed their resources and capabilities to be very sensitive and responsive to differences in local market needs. But this strategic posture has become less important because of converging consumer needs and preferences. The ability to be responsive to differences is still important, however, because it is an important source of innovation.

Specialization of resources has scale economies. But it was risky in an environment which shortened product life cycles and increased changes in costs, tastes, and technologies because it tended to create a rigidity of operations. New flexible manufacturing technologies can overcome the dilemma between scale economies and flexibility.

The issue of decision-making within the transnational company is closely related to the organizational structures which is discussed in Paper 1. In multinational companies, decision-making is decentralized at the level of the foreign subsidiaries which are independence. In global companies, decision-making is centralized at the corporate center and the foreign subsidiaries are dependent.

Independent subsidiaries may be overcome by competitors that can take advantage of scale economies and efficiencies. On the other hand, dependent subsidiaries may result in lack of responsiveness to local market needs and may create political problems with host country governments. Transnational companies may combine centralization and decentralization so as to achieve global coordination and local responsiveness. According to Bartlett and Ghoshal (1989), the management mindset understands the need for multiple strategic capabilities, views problems, and opportunities from both local and global perspectives, and is willing to interact with others openly and flexibly. The task is not to build a sophisticated matrix structure, but to create a "matrix in the minds of managers".

In this book, we investigate whether three major electronics companies in Japan adopt the transnational strategy discussed above or organizational structures and management described in Paper 1.

3   Transnational Strategy and International Management Accounting Systems

International management accounting systems should provide useful information for a worldwide company to execute its strategies and management. When the company adopts a transnational strategy, the company actually tries to achieve global scale economic efficiency, local responsiveness, and organizational learning simultaneously in its worldwide operations.

The company with a transnational strategy centralizes some resources and capabilities in home operations and distributes others among its many national operations. The company should be the integrated network to integrate the specialized and distributed configuration of resources and to build cooperation among interdependent units. Therefore, it is essential for the international management accounting system to communicate information necessary for executing strategies and management among foreign subsidiaries and from foreign subsidiaries to headquarters and vice versa.

The integrated network of distributed resources allows companies to achieve the efficiency of specialization without suffering various disruptions of centralization. Transnational companies can sense potential opportunities and problems from both local and global perspectives and respond to the changes in exchange rates, tastes, technologies, and others. But these characteristics of the transnational company are also the source of problems that are forces of fragmentation and dissipation.

Such a company may deteriorate into organizational anarchy or suffer from centrifugal forces. In order to cope with the greatest problems, the transnational company should provide a sense of unity, trying to ensure that its individual managers share an understanding of the company's purpose and values, an identification with broader goals, and commitment to the overall corporate agenda (Bartlett and Ghoshal, 1989).

To achieve this, Bartlett and Ghoshal (1989) suggested building a shared vision, developing individual understanding and acceptance, and co-opting management efforts (the binding commitment). Their views are summarized as follows.

1. *Building a shared vision*
As the strategic task is more complex and changeable, and the organizational units are more dispersed, and differentiated, individual managers are more likely to become confused. Worldwide companies force managers worldwide to understand a well-articulated corporate vision and broader goals, to commit to consistent implementation, and to share the vision.

Managers in large worldwide companies tend to specialize in one activity and to become narrow and parochial. A well-articulated corporate vision provides these managers with a broader frame of reference that gives context and meaning to their particular roles and responsibilities.

To be an effective shared corporate vision, it should be clearly articulated and communicated to managers worldwide. Even the effective shared corporate vision can dissipate if managers do not commit to consistent implementation of it. Finally, it is essential to establish a consistency of purpose across organizational units. In other words, the vision must be shared by all.

2. Developing individual understanding and acceptance
Most managers in large worldwide companies tend to focus one aspect of the overall corporate task. Even if they intellectually understand the broader objectives implied by the corporate vision, it is difficult for them to internalize the expensive perspective because of their constrained organizational view and narrow experience base.

The lack of managers' understanding and acceptant of the international activities is a barrier to development of a transnational company. As managers at all levels and across all functions must make decisions with important worldwide activities, transnational companies must develop the perspectives of individual managers making such decisions.

As it is essential for managers to have their abilities to perform key roles in international operations, the recruiting and selection process is very important. Furthermore, the use of training and development programs to broaden managers' perspectives is particularly important.

Although recruitment and training are valuable, the best way to broaden managers' perspectives is through personal experience. By moving selected managers across functions, between businesses, and local subsidiaries, individual managers can develop their experiences and perspectives necessary to flexible management.

3. Achieving the active involvement and personal commitment of managers
Although most managers may intellectually understand the corporate vision and have the training to broaden their perspectives, they are so consumed by their immediate operations that they tend to become narrow and parochial when global issues arise. If the worldwide company gives its managers direct responsibility for achieving the corporate vision and key roles in coordinating it, it co-opts them.

4. A matrix in the minds of managers

As companies move toward an integrated network, managers are eager for the necessary structural and systems changes. But it is very important not to change the structure into a matrix but to create a matrix in the minds of managers. In other words, it is necessary to enhance managers' abilities to make such judgments and trade-offs in a way that achieves the corporate vision.

The above-mentioned characteristics of managers are applicable to accountants in the transnational company. The recruiting and selection process and the training and development programs are particularly important to develop accountants' understanding and acceptant for achieving a corporate vision and broader goals. This means that accountants gain a better understanding of local and global accounting issues. Also, accountants must understand transnational strategy and a way that contributes to achieve its strategy by an effective international management accounting system.

According to Kaplan and Norton (2001), the balanced scorecard which is a descriptive and not a prescriptive framework can describe and communicate transnational strategy for all managers. The balanced scorecard measures a company's performance from four perspectives: financial, customer, internal process, and learning and growth from which the strategy used for value creation is described.

The vision creates the picture of the destination or a desirable but uncertain future position. The strategy defines the logic of how this vision will be achieved (Kaplan and Norton, 2001). As the organization has never been to the future position, it must create a series of linked hypotheses. Therefore, the key for implementing strategy is to have everyone in the organization clearly understand the underlying hypotheses, to align resources with the hypotheses, to test the hypotheses continually, and to adapt as required in real time (Kaplan and Norton, 2001).

The balanced scorecard which is a new system for managing strategy must be linked to another system (the budget) for managing tactics. According to Kaplan and Norton (2001), companies can follow an analogous step-down procedure to make the transition from high-level strategy to budgeting for local operations:

(1) Translate strategy into a balanced scorecard, defining the strategic objectives and measures.
(2) Set stretch targets for specific future times for each measure. Identify planning gaps to motivate and stimulate creativity.

(3) Identify strategic initiatives and resource requirements to close the planning gaps, thereby enabling the stretch targets to be achieved.

(4) Authorize financial and human resources for the strategic initiatives. Embed these requirements into the annual budget. The annual budget comprises two components: a strategic budget to manage discretionary programs and an operating budget to manage the efficiency of department, functions, and line items.

The balanced scorecard starts with the destination of four perspectives, charts the routes that will lead there and measures a company's performance. International management accounting systems provide useful information to set targets for specific future times for the four perspectives, especially a financial perspective, and to measure the performance from four perspectives.

4   Information from International Management Accounting

Every transnational company operates in many counties where there are social, cultural, political, legal, economic, and technological differences. Global operations necessitate dealing in different currencies. The foreign subsidiaries of transnational companies normally keep their accounting records and prepare their financial statements in the currency of the country where they are located.

When transnational companies prepare their consolidated financial statements, the financial statements from individual foreign subsidiaries must be translated from the currency of the foreign country into the currency of the country where the transnational is headquartered based on generally accepted accounting principles.

Though a single currency concept (aggregated information) is utilized for financial reporting in a multicurrency economic environment, a multiple currencies concept (disaggregated information) may be needed for managing global operations. The measurement of usefulness of disaggregated information is examined by Ijiri (1995). As capital is homogeneous, aggregated, and abstract, capital managers such as board members and top executives need aggregate information. But, resources are heterogeneous, disaggregated, and concrete and so managers of resources need disaggregated information.

Multicurrency accounting is an effective tool to manage resources. This multicurrency accounting will be introduced by quoting from the article by Duangploy and Owings (1997).

4.1 *The usefulness of multicurrency accounting*

Duangploy and Owings (1997) introduces multicurrency accounting, compares its reporting capabilities with GAAP, and suggests a means to integrate multicurrency accounting into internal reporting and external reporting as supplemental disclosures.

According to Duangploy and Owings (1997), the dollar is the reporting currency for a US company and would represent the equivalent of all related foreign currencies in financial reports under multicurrency accounting. Foreign currency transactions are recorded in that a separate set of accounts — assets, liabilities, and a balancing equity (spot conversion) account — are used as if the currency constituted a separate reporting equity. The equity account is measured at the spot rate unless the transaction is a forward purchase or sale, in which case a forward rate would be used.

The account balance, debit or credit, in the spot conversion account is used to indicate whether an entity is long or short in a particular currency. If a foreign currency transaction involves only one currency, the assets in that currency will be offset by a liability and there would be no foreign exchange exposure. Accordingly, the spot conversion account does not come into play. The spot conversion account will be affected by a cross-currency transaction.

Duangploy and Owings (1997) present an illustration that the US company has the following financial position on 31 December 1994:

Balance Sheet

Assets		Owner's Equity	
Cash	20,000	Common Stock	50,000
Accounts Receivable	40,000	Retained Earnings	30,000
Plant & Equipment	60,000		
Accumulated Depreciation	(40,000)		
Total Assets	80,000	Total Owner's Equity	80,000

They assume that US MUE obtained a British pound — denominated investment in debt securities of £500, financed by a dollar — denominated note payable of $1,000, when the spot rate was £1 = $2 on 1 January 1995.

Under GAAP, the transaction would be recorded as follows:

Investment in debt security $1,000

    Note payable $1,000

Under multicurrency accounting,

$ Spot conversion account $1,000

    Note payable $1,000

Investment in debt security   £500

    £ Spot conversion account   £500

The investment in debt is not redeemable in dollars, but will be settled in pounds; the note payable will be settled in dollars. This is a cross-currency transaction under multicurrency accounting since the investment in pounds is in a different currency than the dollar currency that financed the investment. Accordingly, the entity is long in pounds and short in dollars and discloses the spot conversion accounts.

Next, they assume that a branch office is opened in Thailand and 50,000 Thai baht is received from the issuance of a baht — denominated note when the exchange rate is $1 = B25 on 1 January 1995.

Under GAAP, the transaction would be recorded as follows:

Investment in Branch $2,000

    Note payable $2,000

Under multicurrency accounting,

Investment in Branch   B50,000

    Note payable   B50,000

In this case, assets and liabilities will have the same command or claim after a change in foreign exchange rate as existed before. The baht spot conversion account is not implemented as there is no exposure to foreign exchange risk. The impact of above transactions in a multicurrency format is presented in Table 1 on 1 January 1995.

The multicurrency balance sheet displays the financial position of each currency as well as the consolidated amount in the US dollar. Every currency other than the US dollar is translated using the spot rates equal to the current exchange rates as of the balance sheet date. Using the current rate is both relevant and objective, because multicurrency accounting places emphasis on currency position.

Multicurrency accounting is an effective tool to present a clear picture of foreign exchange exposure. In addition, it provides useful information to present economic reality in various currencies, as business transactions denominated in foreign currency are recorded and communicated in that currency.

Table 1   Multicurrency accounting balance sheet, 1 January 1995

Assets	$	Pounds	Bahts	Combined ($)
Cash	20,000			20,000
Accounts Receivable	40,000			40,000
Investment in Debt Sec.		500		1,000
Investment in Branch			50,000	2,000
Property, Plant, and Equipment	60,000			60,000
Accumulated Depreciation	(40,000)			(40,000)
Total Assets	80,000	500	50,000	80,000
Liabilities and Owner's Equity				
Notes Payable	1,000			1,000
Common Stock	50,000			50,000
Retained Earnings	30,000			30,000
$/£ Spot Conversion Account	(1,000)	500		
$/B Spot Conversion Account				
Total Liab. and Owner's Equity	80,000	500	50,000	80,000

4.2   *Performance evaluation of an international subsidiary*

The control systems in any organization compare the actual performance with planned performance (goals) so that goals are attained. A key step in the control process is performance evaluation. It encompasses gathering, summarizing, and analyzing information to determine whether goals are achieved or not. This process also includes the performance evaluation of foreign subsidiaries and their managers. Performance evaluation for the manager should be separated from the evaluation of the foreign subsidiary for which he is responsible.

Performance evaluation systems should be constructed by considering the strategic objectives for which the strategic objectives for which the foreign subsidiaries were established. The financial measures used for the performance evaluation of foreign subsidiaries, which were recommended in the literature, are return on investment (ROI) and actual versus budgeted performance (Tufer and Aiken, 1989).

Performance evaluation of foreign subsidiaries is similar to that of domestic units. But, the former includes additional factors not present in the latter. Examples of such factors are foreign currency exchange rates and different inflation rates. Currency fluctuations affect the financial results of foreign subsidiaries. Namely, they create economic fluctuations which affect revenues and expenses even as they are measured in local currency. Devaluations are often accompanied by local inflation. When inflation is the major cause of devaluation and local sales prices are increased at the same rate as inflation, revenues measured in local currency will be maintained. Currency fluctuations affect the financial results of the parent company even if local currency results are not affected.

Therefore, it is important to decide whether performance evaluation is measured by the local or parent currency. As different foreign subsidiaries operate in different environments and compete with local competitors, performance standards should preferably be expressed in the local currency. In this case, fluctuation in exchange rates does not affect the computation for performance measurement. The performance standards are to motivate subsidiary managers toward achieving their objectives based on the subsidiary's local currency. But, the parent management may fail to notice how currency fluctuations affect the financial results of foreign subsidiaries. Also, it is difficult to compare among subsidiaries results which are measured by each local currency.

The parent company's currency may be used when the parent management communicates organization goals and objectives to subsidiary managers. Because the parent management is familiar with the parent company's currency and interested in the parent company's currency results of foreign subsidiaries. The parent management can measure how subsidiary managers maintain their amounts of capital investment based on the parent company's currency and motivate subsidiary managers toward improving their financial condition based on the parent company's currency.

Each subsidiary manager has incentives to increase liabilities denominated in the local currency and to decrease local currency assets in devaluation of the local currency because he perceives that his success is tied to the income results for his operations. This may be in conflict with parent goals and objectives as the parent management may deem it appropriate for the company to maintain a constant level of current ratio.

When subsidiary manager is relieved of all responsibility for foreign exchange exposure, he should not be evaluated on the parent currency results being influenced by exchange risk policies over whose effect he has little control. A foreign subsidiary's performance should be evaluated on its contributions as an entity toward achieving the parent company's goal and objectives. On the other hand, a subsidiary manager participates in setting the performance criteria and should be evaluated on factors he can control.

Indeed, the major global issue in budgeting for a transnational company is to determine the currency in which the budget is prepared: the local currency or the parent company's currency. In budgeting for a transnational company that uses the parent company's currency, there is a need to translate the budgets of foreign subsidiaries into the parent currency. It is important to determine the foreign exchange rates in the budgeting process as it relates to the performance evaluation of subsidiary managers.

4.3   *Budget management and foreign exchange rates*

If centralized management decisions are imposed on subsidiary managers, and if the effects of such decisions are not eliminated from the performance evaluation, performance standards will not provide accurate guides for control and motivate subsidiary managers. On the other hand, if subsidiary managers are given all responsibility for each subsidiary foreign management decision, they will not follow policies which are optimal from the company viewpoint, if the policies may make their results worse.

Lessard and Lorange (1977) introduce the question of an appropriate exchange rate for use in the budgeting process. Namely, they identify the different ways that companies can translate the budget from the local currency into the parent currency and then monitor actual performance.

In dealing with foreign exchange rates in the budgeting process as it relates to performance evaluation of managers, three different exchange rates are incorporated at two points: (1) in setting the operating budget for a particular time period, and (2) in tracking realized performance relative to the budget (Lessard and Lorange, 1977).

The first is the actual (spot) rate at the time when the budget was set, the second is the rate that was projected for the end of the period at the time when the budget was set in the local currency, and the third is the actual rate at the end of the period. The combinations of these three rates in budgeting process are outlined in Figure 1. Four cells are shaded out because they are illogical combinations.

Rate Used to Track Performance Relative to Budget / Rate Used for Determining Budget	Actual at Time of Budget	Projected at Time of Budget	Actual at End of Period
Actual at time of budget	A-1	A-2	A-3
Projected at time of budget	P-1	P-2	P-3
Actual at end of period (through updating)	E-1	E-2	E-3

Fig. 1   Possible combinations of exchange rates in the control process

In combination A-1, the actual rate at the time when the budget was set is used in the budget preparation as well as in results relative to the budget. This implicit assumption is that the exchange rate will not change, but if it does, the subsidiary manager is not given responsibility for foreign exchange exposure and his performance evaluation is not affected by it.

In combination A-3, the budget is set at the initial exchange rate, while actual results are translated at the actual rate at the end of the period. When the exchange rate will change, subsidiary manager is given responsibility for the effect of any changes.

In combination P-2, a projected exchange rate is used both in the budget preparation and in translating the actual results. The subsidiary manager is given responsibility for performance defined at that rate regardless of the actual outcome. According to Lessard and Lorange (1977), the projected rates used in the budgeting process are referred to internal forward rates (IFRs) since their use is analogous to the treasurer acting as a banker and "buying forward" receipts in foreign currencies at a guaranteed rate.

In combination P-3, the budget is set at the projected exchange rate and the actual results are translated at the actual rate at the end of the period. This holds the subsidiary manager responsible for the impact on performance of deviations from the projected exchange rate. In this case, the treasurer does not "guarantee" the forward rate.

In combination E-3, the actual exchange rate at the end of the period is used both in the budget preparation and in translating of the actual results. This does not hold the subsidiary manager responsible for any exchange rate fluctuation since the budget is always updated as the exchange rate changes.

Combinations A-1 and E-3 allow the subsidiary manager to ignore the effect of any fluctuations in the exchange rate. Combination A-3 attributes the impact of exchange fluctuations to the subsidiary manager at the time of translating actual results. Each subsidiary manager will take hedging actions to reduce exchange risks from a local perspective. These actions may not be optimal from the company viewpoint.

Lessard and Lorange (1977) pointed out as follows: combination P-2 generally will be superior to all others and the procedure of using IFRs as the basis for decision-making and performance evaluation satisfies two major criteria for good management control systems, goal-congruence, and fairness.

Goal-congruence is kept because the treasurer projects IFRs from the company viewpoint and subsidiary managers take the responsibility for performance at IFRs to achieve company goals and objectives. Fairness is kept because performance evaluation of subsidiary is the assessment of how the subsidiary carries out company goals and objectives on the basis of IFRs which subsidiary managers participate in setting.

4.4   *Need for composite currency*

Implicit in the budgeting control of global companies are assumptions about use of the parent company's currency. Therefore, I discussed the question of an appropriate exchange rate for use in setting the budget and in tracking realized performance relative to budget.

But, Ijiri (1995) pointed out as follows:

Use of the currency of the parent company's home country is most common. This is proper only as long as the company's foreign investments are temporary. Global companies invest in foreign countries semi-permanently and operate all over the world providing a great degree of coordination and integration of their worldwide activities. For these global companies, use of the parent company's currency in foreign currency translation does not make sense.

The performance of a foreign subsidiary is assessed by the extent of its contributions to achieve the company goals and objectives. If it is the company objective to repatriate all foreign subsidiaries into the parent company's home country, the parent company's currency should be used as the reporting currency.

However, the global company locates its value-chain activities based on lower costs as well as on the potential for creating additional value for its products or services anywhere in the world. In other words, it locates foreign subsidiaries near cheaper and high-quality resources, centers of research and innovation, and key customers. Therefore, it holds assets and liabilities denominated in multiple currencies throughout the world and deals in different national currencies. Business transactions denominated in a local currency are recorded in that currency.

Such a global company sets its objectives which are quantified in terms of multiple currencies as well as a composite currency. If the objective is to maintain investments in different national currencies at a certain ratio, the composite currency should be used as the reporting currency.

According to Ijiri (1995), a composite currency should be chosen among alternatives in such a way that the composition of individual currencies in the portfolio of the composite currency closely approximates the target asset holding of corporation in the respective country. In this way, the investors are accurately informed of the progress made by the corporation along the growth line dictated by its objective.

Example. If the company objective is to hold yen and dollar which consists of ¥100 and $1 and to develop at the ratio, a composite currency consists of ¥100 and $1, that is:

$$G1 = (¥100, \$1).$$

The composition of G1 remains constant regardless of the fluctuation in the exchange rate between the two currencies. If the objective is to gain the profits of G100, it gains the profits of ¥10,000 and $100. A company holds a portfolio of currencies, (¥10,000, $100), which is denoted by H:

$$H = (¥10,000, \$100).$$

The holding remains unchanged throughout the year. The exchange rate between yen and dollar changes from ¥100 = $1 at the beginning of the year to ¥200 = $1 at the end of the year. At the beginning of the year, the exchange rate is ¥100 = $1, hence G1 = (¥100, $1), G1 = ¥200 = $2, ¥1= G1/200 and $1 = G1/2, and H = (¥10,000, $100) = ¥10,000×G1/200 + $100×G1/2 = G100. At the end of the year, the exchange rate is ¥200 = $1, hence G1 = (¥100, $1), G1 = ¥300 = $1.5, ¥1= G1/300 and $1 = G1/1.5, and H = (¥10,000, $100) = ¥10,000×G1/300 + $100×G1/1.5 = G100.

As the composite currency consists of multiple currencies at a certain ratio which is congruent with the objective of the company, it is rational to set the plan of the company in terms of the composite currency. The global company must maintain the composition of multiple currencies in the portfolio of the composite currency by setting the plan of each foreign subsidiary in terms of each local currency. It would be ideal for the company as a whole to use the composite currency for its internal performance evaluation.

References

Bartlett, C. A. and Ghoshal, S. (1989). *Managing Across Borders: The Transnational Solution*, Harvard Business School Press.

Cullen, J. B. and Parboteeah, K. P. (2005). *Multinational Management: A Strategic Approach*, South-Western.

Duangploy, O. and Owings, G. W. (1997). The compatibility of multicurrency accounting with functional currency accounting, *The International Journal of Accounting* 32(4), pp. 441–462.

Ijiri, Y. (1995). Global financial reporting using a composite currency: An aggregation theory perspective, *The International Journal of Accounting* 30(1), pp. 95–106.

Kaplan, R. S. and Norton, D. P. (2001). *The Strategy-Focused Organization*, Harvard Business School Press.

Lessard, D. R. and Lorange, P. (1977). Currency changes and management control: Resolving the centralization/decentralization dilemma, *The Accounting Review* 52(3), pp. 628–637.

Tufer, A. C. and Aiken, L. A. (1989). Performance evaluation techniques for international operations: Impacts on managerial incentives and strategic planning considerations, in *Managerial Accounting and Analysis in Multinational Enterprises*, edited by Holzer, H. P. and Schoenfeldin, H. W., Walter de Gruyter & Co., pp. 163–173.

Yip, G. S. (1992). *Total Global Strategy: Managing for Worldwide Competitive Advantage*, Prentice Hall.

Part 2

Current Status of International Management Accounting

The Actual Conditions of International Management Accounting in Matsushita Electric Industrial Co., Ltd.

Asako Kimura

Associate Professor, Faculty of Business Administration
Kyushu Sangyo University

Takahisa Toyoda

Planning and Control Group
Nihon Spindle Manufacturing Co., Ltd.

1   Matsushita Electric Industrial Company (Panasonic)

1.1   *Founding*

At the time it was founded, Matsushita Electric Industrial Company (abbreviated as Matsushita below) had just three employees. Now, the employees number 328,645 and the capital has risen to 258.74 billion yen (as of 31 March 2007), and Matsushita has grown to a company that is representative of the Japanese electronics industry. In 1920, a presence was established in Tokyo to extend sales to that region. In 1922, a head office and factory were completed and, at that stage, Matsushita Electric had succeeded in developing from a cottage industry into small enterprise with 50 employees. In 1929, the name was changed to Matsushita Electric Manufacturing Company and the general plan for Matsushita Electric's path into the future was decided. That plan, with subsequent modifications, has evolved into the company's present plan ("Devote ourselves to our vocations as workers in industry, strive to improve life in society, and contribute to the development of world culture"). Also, in the same year, a second office and factory were being completed.

By 1932, Matsushita Electric had grown into a company that had over 1,200 employees, and more than 200 products. In the following year, a third office and factory were completed in Kadoma, the location of the current head office. In that year, Matsushita Electric introduced an original autonomous division corporate structure. The autonomous divisions of that time were the Radio Division, the Lamp and Battery Division, and the Wiring, Plastics and Electric Heating Division, which allowed independence in responsibility and management by product area. Overleaf, we describe the history of Matsushita up to the present (Matsushita Electric Industrial Company website, 2007; Miyamoto, 1992; Miyamoto, 1997) (Table 1).

1.2   *Post-war reconstruction and the major push overseas*

The 39 overseas factories and sales offices were reduced to 17 (of which six were factories) when the war ended in 1945. Those, however, were confiscated by the opposing countries, and Matsushita Electric's overseas activities ceased until the re-opening of trade after the war. In 1935, Matsushita Electric Manufacturing was reorganized into Matsushita Electric Industries. At that time, a subsidiary organization that had evolved from the autonomous division organization was adopted, and the autonomous divisions were re-established as nine subsidiary companies.

After defeat in the war, Matsushita Electric was confronted with the greatest crisis since its establishment as a result of the order from General Headquarters of the occupation forces to halt production and their policy of dissolving the zaibatsu. However, that problem was surmounted with the solidarity of labor unions and other such organizations in 1946. Later, in 1949, the manufacturing mechanism was abolished, factories were reformed to a system of individual profitability, and production was fully rationalized. Then, in 1950, another restructuring again brought a major reformation, with a restoration of the traditional autonomous division system based on thorough rationalization of production by individual profitability of factories.

In 1951, Corporate President Konosuke Matsushita made his first visit to the United States to look into overseas expansion. With that trip, Mr. Matsushita became determined to expand overseas, and Matsushita Electric Industries was set up in co-operation with the Phillips Company of Holland in 1952. Along with that, Matsushita Electric Industries built new factories of world-leading technological standards and scale. The first period of construction was completed in 1954. Production began with light bulbs and fluorescent lamps, and later included vacuum tubes, cathode ray tubes, transistors, and semiconductors. Those electron tubes and semiconductors were used to raise the world level of every kind of electronic product.

Table 1   History of Matsushita

Year	
1918	Konosuke Matsushita founds Matsushita Electric Devices Manufacturing Works
1932	International trade division created
1933	Business division system adopted
1935	Matsushita Electric Trading Company established Incorporated as Matsushita Electric Industries (capitalized at 1 billion yen)
1949	Listed on the Tokyo Stock Exchange and the 0 saka Stock Exchange
1952	Matsushita DenshiKogyo (KK) set up through technical collaboration with Philips of the Netherlands; four vacuum tube factories split off
1959	Matsushita Electric Corporation of America now Panasonic Corporation North America) established, followed by various other overseas manufacturing and marketing companies
1971	Listed on the New York Stock Exchange
1975	100 millon USD (parvalae) in convertible corporate bonds issued
1981	Overseas Corporate Headquarters set up
1983	ACTEN 21 three-year plan initiated
1985	Panasonic Finance, Inc. was set up in the U.S.
1988	Merger with Matsushita Electric Trading Company (KK)
1990	Acquisition of MCA, the U.S. entertainment company
1993	Affiliation between Matsushita DenshiKogyo (KK) and Philips dissolved and Philips sells off all stock holding Matsushita DenshiKogyo (KK)
1995	Transfer of 80% of U.S. subsidiary holdings in MCA to Seagram of Canada
2002	Matsushita Communications (KK), Kyushu Matsushita Electric (KK), Matsushita Seiko (KK,) Matsushita Shkoku Panasonic (KK) and Matsushita Power Transmission Systems (KK) made wholly-owned subsidiaries through a stock
2003	Structal change to management by business domain Merger of Group company Matsushita Electric (KK) and Matsushita Power Transmission Systems (KK) Matsushita Electronic Components (KK) and Matsushita Battery Industrial (KK) made wholly-owned subsidiaries through stock swap Panasonic is made the globalbrand
2006	A11 U.S. subsidiary holdings in Universal Studios (formerly MCA) transferred to Vivendi

Concerning sales, in 1950 the sales companies system was started in some regions, and in the following year, the company proceeded with consolidation of the main office sales staff department and expansion of regional sales offices. The establishment of sales companies in various locations throughout Japan was actively promoted until 1959. The vigorous cultivation of overseas markets also began in 1951. In August 1951, Matsushita Electric Trading, which had been made independent in the post-war dissolution of the Matsushita Electric Group, once again came under the management umbrella of Matsushita Electric. At the same time, employees were sent to Southeast Asia, the Middle East, South America, and other regions to develop export routes. In addition, a branch office was opened in New York in 1953 to investigate foreign technological and market trends and to establish an office for overseas expansion.

After 1955, an improving standard of living in Japan raised the demand for household electrical appliances. In 1956, monochrome TVs, washing machines, and refrigerators had become known as "the three treasures". Along with that increase in demand, Matsushita Electric expanded its field of business, and its 11 divisions were divided into 15 divisions in 1956. Then, new factories were built one after the other, and genuine mass production began.

Concerning the promotion of exports, even greater effort was expected of Matsushita Electric Trading, and the New York branch office was bolstered in September 1959 to build an independent overseas sales network for Matsushita Electric and to popularize the company's products. In addition, Matsushita Electric USA was established as a local sales company. In November 1959, an international head office was established to invigorate overseas activities, including the export of materials as well as products. By strengthening the export organization in this way, Matsushita Electric exports increased from 3.2 billion yen in 1958 to 13.0 billion yen in 1960. Moreover, the proportion of exports to total production increased from 6% to 12% in that time period.

1.3 *Factory development and strengthening of overseas sales networks*

At the beginning of 1961, there was an effort to increase exports based on the policy of "Take a global viewpoint and work with the entire world in mind", and technical assistance to various countries and active building of overseas factories were begun. First, in 1961, technical assistance concerning radio assembly was given to local industries in Pakistan, South Vietnam, and Uruguay, and National Thailand was established in Thailand as the first overseas manufacturing company after the war, with a 60% investment. Technical assistance was given, and local production of batteries began. Then, from 1962 to 1968, overseas manufacturing companies were established one after another in Taiwan, Malaysia, Mexico, Puerto Rico, Peru, Costa Rica, Tanzania, Brazil, the Philippines, and Australia. During that period in the mid-1960s, market conditions in Japan deteriorated with the tightening of credit. Nevertheless, Matsushita Electric overcame that problem through its own effort, and based on the business philosophy of Matsushita Electric, all of the overseas manufacturing companies were operated under the basic policy of contributing to the prosperity of the host countries. The term "own effort" means as follow. Reflecting on the words "Up to now, the operations departments, business offices and sales companies have all experienced prosperous conditions and tend to rely on each other, and we have lost the spirit of independent hard work and ambition", Matsushita Electric implemented a new sales organization in 1965. It consisted essentially of (1) consolidating and strengthening a national network of sales companies; (2) direct sales by the operations departments, without going through the business offices; and (3) a new monthly sales system. Within Matsushita Electric, too, in addition to instilling independence and responsibility in management and strengthening a product development organization that is directly linked to sales, there was a comprehensive reformation of the management system to provide a support structure for sales companies and retail outlets.

In parallel with exporting and technical assistance, progress was also made in setting up an overseas sales network, and there were over 100 overseas representative offices in 1963. Following Matsushita Electric USA, the establishment of overseas sales companies was also stepped up from 1962 on. In that year, Hamburg Matsushita Electric was established in West Germany a branch office for movement into Europe. Following that, Matsushita Electric Trading opened representative offices in 10 countries, including Australia and France, and further set up new sales companies in Hawaii, Peru, Canada, Costa Rica, Brazil, and other countries. With that activity, exports increased to exceed 33.0 billion yen in 1965 and reached 67.7 billion yen in 1967.

In 1968, there were 12 overseas manufacturing companies and seven sales companies for a total of 19 overseas companies. In that year, Matsushita Electric celebrated the 50th anniversary of its founding and further sharpened its global management strategy. In 1968, a manufacturing company was set up in Venezuela and a sales company was established in Mexico, pushing exports to over 100 billion yen. In 1970, two manufacturing companies were set up, National Global (Indonesia) and Philips Matsushita Battery Corporation (Belgium). In addition to those, one sales company was set up in Thailand and two were established in Panama. In 1971, the company was listed on the New York Stock Exchange. Then, in 1972, more overseas manufacturing companies were established, one in Singapore, two in Malaysia, and three in Indonesia, and sales companies were set up in Sweden, the United Kingdom, Italy, and West Germany. Thus, there were 22 overseas manufacturing companies and 15 sales companies in 1972, for a total of 37 overseas companies. Furthermore, in 1973, manufacturing companies were set up in Korea, Spain, and Iran, and sales companies were established in Venezuela, El Salvador, Belgium, and Brazil. As a result, Matsushita then had 25 overseas manufacturing companies and 19 overseas sales companies, for a total of 44 overseas companies. In that same year, the company gained listing on stock markets on the U.S. west coast, Amsterdam, Frankfurt, Düsseldorf, Hong Kong, and Paris. In 1973, the company issued 100 million dollars worth of convertible corporate bonds denominated in US dollars, mainly in the United States, for international financing. In 1974, manufacturing companies were set up in the United States, England, and Brazil, and sales companies were set up in Singapore, Guatemala, and Belgium, for totals of 28 manufacturing companies and 22 sales companies, and a grand total of 50 overseas companies.

The effects of the sharp rise of the yen following the floating of currency rates in 1973 and the oil shock recession continued into 1975. In response to such changes in the business environment, as a system aiming for even further efficiency of management, Matsushita Electric formed three corporate headquarters (electric machinery, radio equipment, and industrial equipment), with the head of each headquarters acting as President. Together with that reorganization, the divisions and related manufacturing organizations in Japan were brought under the management authority of each headquarters President and their management activities were developed on that basis. In 1976, that organizational system was also applied to the overseas manufacturing companies.

1.4   *Long-term vision guides overseas development*

In 1978, the Japanese economy entered a period of low growth and pending issues such as the high yen and international trade friction meant that it was a period in which Japan faced unclear prospects. Therefore, to avoid distraction by near-future changes as seen from a short-term point of view, a three-year medium-term plan was introduced in the beginning of latter half of 1978, in addition to the traditional yearly business plan. Then, in 1981, Matsushita set a long-term vision that targeted the next 10 years and a more aggressive development of foreign business to accompany Japan's economic growth. The long-term vision aimed for a 50% proportion of overseas business, with 25% from exports and 25% from overseas production for overall high production, placing more emphasis on overseas business.

Following the long-term vision, Matsushita (1) embarked on the path that led it from its base in home appliances toward becoming a general electronics manufacturer, and (2) searched for a path to business development expanding to highly promising products, semiconductors, and industrial products. Of these two directions, the path to becoming a general electronics manufacturer was the more specific, so the three-year ACTION-61 plan was started in 1983. The objectives of the plan were to reform the operational structure and strengthen management, and to strengthen overseas business. The promotion of overseas business was based on a six-point approach: (1) do business that is welcomed by the country; (2) promote business that is in line with the governmental policy of the country; (3) continue to produce products that are competitive internationally in terms of quality, performance, and cost; (4) positively promote the transfer of technology overseas; (5) establish a managerial structure for raising profits and continue internal generation of capital for business expansion; and (6) cultivate local employees.

At the end of 1983, there were 80 overseas companies in 37 countries, including 46 manufacturing companies in 27 countries and 34 marketing companies in 28 countries. At that time, the proportion of overseas companies was 42.7%.

In 1984, the functions of the head office and the overseas regional head offices were transferred to Matsushita Electric Trading. Integrating the organizations of the overseas head offices and Matsushita Electric Trading achieved a strengthening of competitive power by (1) unifying the Matsushita Group's overseas strategy, (2) expediting decisions and actions, and (3) rationalizing total cost. It also achieved the objective of strengthening the overseas departments. In that way, the Matsushita Group was able to achieve its original overseas strategy of unifying overseas production, export, and other overseas business, and making Matsushita Electric Trading the core for promoting and overall development of overseas business. Along with this transfer of control, the new organizational structure of

Matsushita Electric Trading was altered in the following four ways: (1) The marketing division of Matsushita Electric Trading was reorganized into five regional headquarters for North America, Central and South America, Europe, the Asia–Pacific region, and the Near and Middle East and Africa, and the head of each regional office was given the responsibility and authority for promoting overseas business, including export and overseas production; (2) An overseas business promotion department was established in each regional office, and the functions of the head of the overseas supervisory department were transferred to it; (3) The China office and the Tokyo Panasonic office were given parallel responsibilities for the China market and the PX market; (4) Under the regional general director, a regional general office and an overseas public relations department were established. The regional general director of the regional headquarters makes adjustments and assists in matters concerning regional problems.

In the China market, a color cathode ray tube manufacturing company, the Beijing Matsushita Color CRT Company (BMCC), was established in 1987 as Matsushita Electric's first joint venture. The investment was 50% on the Matsushita side (Matsushita Electric and Matsushita Electric Industries) and 50% on the China side. That was followed by vigorous business expansion with the rapid growth in the Chinese market in the 1990s, and by April 2001, 44 local companies had been set up.

In 1988, three points were raised as a managerial policy: (1) promote internationalization, (2) strengthen technological capabilities, and (3) challenge important business. Currently, the overseas companies include 60 manufacturing companies, 37 sales companies, and four finance companies, for a total of 101 companies. In April 1988, Matsushita Electric merged with Matsushita Electric Trading to promote business from a more global point of view. By doing so, a new internationally oriented start was made, but the emphasis was on (1) establishing an overseas foundation, (2) promoting internationalization from within, and (3) the important challenge of harmony with the world and co-existence. In October of that year, for a more thorough localization of overseas business, regional headquarters were set up for the three regions of the United States, Europe and Africa, and Asia and the Near and Middle East, along with an International Commerce Headquarters that was under the direct control of the President. In addition, an Overseas Production Promotion Department, an International Personnel Department, and a Foreign Exchange Department were established, and a new Overseas Public Relations Department was set up under the Public Relations Headquarters and a new Overseas Planning Department was set up under the Public Relations Division. Concerning imports, the economic friction surrounding Japan increased in severity in July 1989. The International Co-operation Action Plan was announced in September 1989, the International Co-operation Promotion Department was set up, and proactive activities were developed with the objective of balanced internationalization resting on the three pillars of (1) expansion of imports, (2) expansion of overseas production, and (3) expansion of internal demand.

1.5 *Post-bubble slump*

The collapse of the Japanese economic bubble in 1990 was accompanied by a severe recession. The demand in the electronics industry also slumped, creating difficult management problems for Matsushita. In 1993, Yoichi Morishita assumed the position of CEO and undertook an aggressive restructuring of Matsushita under the slogan "Creation and Challenge".

In 1997, Matsushita launched a global restructuring of management based on a medium-term plan named Development 2000, and introduced a new autonomous division structure within the company. At that time, Matsushita had a divisional structure, a system which Matsushita had a hand in introducing for the first time in Japan in 1933. The objectives of introducing autonomous divisions were (1) rapid advance in technology, (2) product fusion and compositing, and (3) coping with the circumstances of business globalization, consolidation as a "business group" business divisions that should cooperate in business activities on the basis of a single management vision to rapidly promote strategic management. The four single operational units set up as autonomous divisions were AVC, Home Electronics, Air Conditioning, and Motors. Operations were based on four points: (1) the same positioning as the current autonomous divisions, with the same structure and operations as independent corporations; (2) the autonomous division as the basic unit for the managerial responsibility system, business planning, and accounting studies and reports; (3) management as the responsibility of the CEO of each autonomous division, and optimum management performed according to the discretion of the CEO; and (4) the autonomous department as the basis for the structure within an autonomous division. This organizational restructuring was inherited by the next CEO of the company, Kunio Nakamura.

2   Organizational Structure and Business Administration

2.1   *Restructuring for recovery from a slump*

Inheriting the restructuring direction established by Morishita, CEO Nakamura began a new system in 2000. CEO Nakamura appealed for the importance of moving toward Morishita's '21st Century-style "super-manufacturing"', which made full use of information technology, and toward a "flat and wavy" organizational structure in which all employees on all levels of the company meet face-to-face with customers. In November 2000, the outline of the three-year Value Creation 21 business plan that was to begin after 2001 was announced (Matsushita Corporation, 2002, 2003, 2004).

Under Nakamura's management, the firm size of Matsushita was as below. The data in Figure 1 is on consolidated basis. In 2001, Matsushita experienced its first operating loss since the company was established.

According to Nakamura, the reasons for the deficit were: (1) a decline in demand both within Japan and overseas in 2001; (2) falling prices due to severe competition; (3) a one-time expense associated with down-sizing (approximately 164.0 billion yen); (4) depreciation of facilities accompanying reorganization, etc.; and (5) depreciation of stock value due to deteriorating stock market conditions (approximately 92.8 billion yen) (Matsushita Electric Industrial Company, 2002 first-quarter stock report).

The founder, Konosuke Matsushita, has been referred to in Japan as an economic god and is known as a man who never approved of a reduction in personnel. Many regarded the down-sizing of Matsushita as a repudiation of the founder, and the reform by Nakamura was regarded critically by many in the mass media (*Weekly Toyo Keizai*, 2001; *Weekly Diamond*, 2001; *Nikkei Business*, 2001; *Economist*, 2002).

Nevertheless, Nakamura did not relent in his reform. He carried out the Value Creation 21 plan with a strong will and went further to promote the Leap Ahead 21 plan. Together with the restructuring, he also carried out positive reorganization and management reform. The efforts bore fruit in the balance sheets from 2002 on as steadily increasing sales and operating income. Nakamura produced results to match his words.

The purpose of this paper is to consider and discuss Nakamura's reformation from the viewpoint of international management and accounting. We therefore begin with an outline of the Value Creation 21 plan and the Leap Ahead 21 plan, which was implemented as a three-year plan that commenced in 2004.

Capital

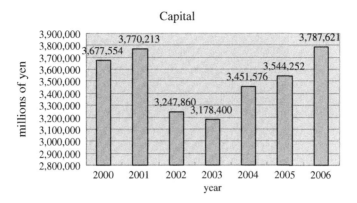

Employee number

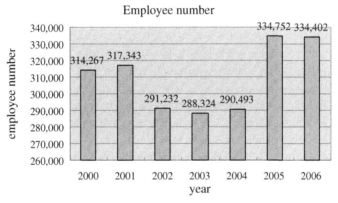

Sales

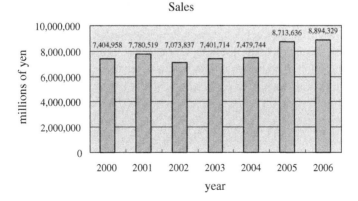

Fig. 1   Various data of Matsushita
Source: Matsushita Corporation (2004, 2005, 2006).

Operating profit

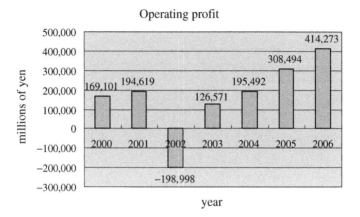

Fig. 1   (*Continued*)

The objective of the Value Creation 21 plan was to execute "deconstruction and creation" (restructuring of the entire company and formulating and executing a growth strategy for the entire company for reformation toward "super-manufacturing", to create a new Matsushita that could contribute to society in the 21st century as well). The targets for 2003 were set at (1) profitability: consolidated operating income rate of 5% or more, (2) capital profitability: capital cost management (CCM) of zero or more, and (3) growth: consolidated sale of nine trillion yen.

Next, the Leap Ahead 21 plan was basically a continuation of the Value Creation 21 plan. It involved strengthening management through acceleration of growth by putting V products on the market, and by a thorough slimming of assets, process reform to make the most use of information technology, and continuing with selective and focused business investment.

The two overall corporate objectives of the Leap Ahead 21 plan, following the Value Creation 21 plan, are (1) secure a CCM of zero or more for all business domain companies by 2005, and (2) attain operating profit of 5% or more and a consolidated CCM of zero or more for the entire company in 2006.

2.2   *Reformation of organizational structure and management*

CEO Nakamura accomplished the restructuring described overleaf while in office (*Weekly Diamond*, 2004). His main outcomes are shown in Figure 2. In the 2001 reformation, offices in Japan and abroad were streamlined, the

Year	Month	Event
2000	6	Kunio Nakamura becomes CEO
	6	Revision of domestic Matsushita Power Transmission Systems production system with closure of two facilities
	10	Matsushita Plasma Displays (KK) established by joint investment with Toray (25%)
2001	1	Absorption of Matsushita Denshi Kogyo (now Panasonic Electronic Devices)
	1	Operation of U.S. air conditioner compressor factory halted
	4	Start of the Value Creation 21 plan
	4	Restructuring of home appliance distribution and establishment of the Marketing Head Office
	8	Cooperation with NEC on next-generation cell phone
	9	Acceptance of Special Life Plan Assistance Program applications begins
	10	Announcement of integration of LCD business with Toshiba
	10	Announcement of new cathode ray tube materials company established by joint purchase with Toshiba
	11	Dissolution of U.K. cell phone company
2002	1	Announcement of converting 5 group companies to wholly-owned subsidiaries by stock swap
	1	Special Life Plan Assistance Program applications ended
	4	Agreement for cooperation in home appliances with the TCL Group
	4	Announcement of Matsushita Group restructuring
	4	Merger of Kysuhu Matsushita Electric and Matsushita Power Transmission Systems
	9	Matsushita Electronic Components and Matsushita Battery Industrial made wholly-owned subsidiaries
	9	Integration of cathode ray tube business with Toshiba
	10	Conversion of 5 group companies to wholly-owned subsidiaries completed
2003	1	New business structure introduced (domain system)
	4	New management system introduced
	4	Panasonic chosen as the unified global brand
	8	Integration of four products by Minebea–Matsushita Motor Corporation announced
	12	Announcement of changing Matsushita Electric Industries to a subsidiary by TOB
2004	4	Integration of air conditioning company into Matsushita Home Appliances
	4	Unification of Matsushita Electric Industries and Matsushita Denko brands
	4	Matsushita Electric Industries made a subsidiary by TOB completion
	6	Consolidation of automotive electronics production facilities in Japan
	6	Consolidation of cell phone production facilities in Japan
2005	4	Matsushita Industrial Equipment Group dissolved and the subsidiaries integrated
	4	Matsushita Shikoku Kogyo changed to Panasonic Shikoku Electronics

Fig. 2   Main changes in the organization of the Matsushita Group by Nakamura
Source: *Weekly Diamond* (2004).

domestic home appliance distribution was restructured, and employee hiring was reformed without regard for any sacred cow. A new framework was constructed through reconsideration of the previous management systems. At that same time, reformation of the production process to make best use of information technology and reformation of the research, development, and design system through construction of a technology platform system, and rationalization of costs by promotion of centralization, unification, and standardization were promoted.

From 2002 to 2003, the Matsushita Group was restructured. In October 2002, five Group companies (Matsushita Communication Systems (KK), Kyushu Matsushita Electrical Company (KK), Matsushita Seiko Company (KK), Matsushita Home Appliance Industries (KK), and Matsushita Power Transmission Systems (KK)) were made wholly owned subsidiaries by an exchange of securities. This essential absorption of listed subsidiary corporations was expected to be difficult from the beginning. For example, the price per share of Matsushita Communication Systems (KK) was 15,000 yen, so the acquisition was very difficult even from a financial standpoint. Nevertheless, by introducing goodwill accounting according to the standards of the U.S. Securities and Exchange Committee rather than the market stock price, the market value was suppressed and acquisition as a wholly owned subsidiary was achieved.

This Group re-organization is illustrated in Figure 3. In the new domain system, the segments are as shown in Figures 4 and 5.

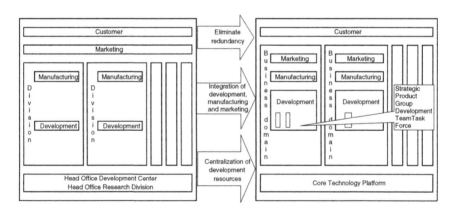

Fig. 3   Re-organization of the Matsushita Group
Source: Matsushita Corporation (2006).

SEGMENTS	BUSINESS DOMAINS	BUSINESS DOMAIN COMPANIES AND GROUP COMPANIES	MAIN PRODUCTS
AVC Networks	• AVC • Fixed-line Communications • Mobile Communications • Automotive Electronics • System Solutions	• Panasonic AVC Networks Company • Panasonic Communications Co., Ltd. • Panasonic Mobile Communications Co., Ltd. • Panasonic Automotive Systems Company • Panasonic System Solutions Company • Matsushita Kotobuki Electronics Industries, Ltd.	Color TVs, PDP and liquid crystal display (LCD) TVs, VCRs, camcorders, digital cameras, DVD players/recorders, compact disc (CD), Mini Disc (MD) and SD players, other personal and home audio equipment, AV and computer product devices, broadcast- and business-use AV equipment and systems, PCs, CD-ROM, DVD-ROM/RAM and other optical disk drives, SD Memory Cards, copiers, printers, telephones, cellular phones, facsimile equipment, car AVC equipment, traffic-related systems, communications network-related equipment, other information and communications equipment and systems, etc.

Home Appliances	• Home Appliances
	• Household Equipment
	• Healthcare Systems
	• Lighting
	• Environmental Systems
		• Home Appliances Group
		  • Matsushita Home Appliances Company
		  • Packaged Air-Conditioner Company
		  • Matsushita Refrigeration Company
		• Healthcare Business Company
		• Lighting Company
		• Matsushita Ecology Systems Co., Ltd.
			Refrigerators, room air conditioners, washing machines, clothes dryers, vacuum cleaners, electric irons, microwave ovens, cooking appliances, dishwasher/dryers, electric fans, air purifiers, heating equipment, kitchen fixture systems, electric, gas and kerosene hot water supply equipment, bath and sanitary equipment, healthcare equipment, electric lamps, ventilation and air-conditioning equipment, car air conditioners, compressors, vending machines, etc.

Components and Devices	• Semiconductors • Display Devices • Batteries • Electronic Components • Electric Motors	• Semiconductor Company • Matsushita Battery Industrial Co., Ltd. • Matsushita Electronic Components Co., Ltd. • Motor Company • Others	Semiconductors, CRTs, LCD panels, PDPs, general components (capacitors, resistors, coils, speakers, power supplies, electro-mechanical components, high frequency components, printed circuit boards, etc.), magnetic recording heads, electric motors, dry batteries, rechargeable batteries, etc.
JVC		• Victor Company of Japan, Ltd.	VCRs, camcorders, color TVs, stereo hi-fi and related equipment, car audio, DVD players, DVD recorders, CD radio cassette recorders, business- and education-use equipment, information equipment, KARAOKE systems, video projectors, display components, optical pickups, motors, high-density multi-layered printed circuit boards, AV software for DVD, CD and video tapes, etc.

Other	• Factory Automation	• Panasonic Factory Solutions Co., Ltd.
		• Matsushita Industrial Equipment Group
		  • Matsushita Industrial Information Equipment Co., Ltd.
		  • Matsushita Welding Systems Co., Ltd.
		• Others
			Electronic-parts-mounting machines, industrial robots, electronic measuring instruments, welding equipment, power distribution equipment, elevators, escalators, bicycles, leasing and credit operations, imported materials and components, certain MEW products, etc.

Fig. 4   Business segment classifications
Source: Matsushita Corporation (2006).

The features of this new organization are empowerment and capital governance. The result of the transfer of authority is that each business domain company bears all of the authority and responsibility for the business in its domain, and the head office monitors the management from the viewpoint of a dividend-earning shareholder. This is so that each business domain

AVC Network • Sales

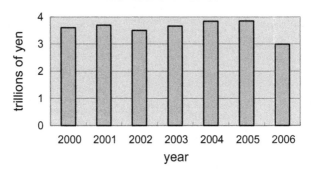

Year	Sales
2002	3,508,624
2003	3,668,195
2004	3,840,268
2005	3,858,781
2006	2,986,088

AVC Network • Profit (Loss)

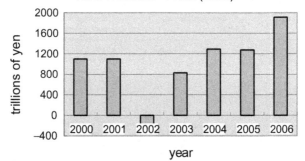

Year	Profit (Loss)
2002	(35,625)
2003	82,828
2004	129,102
2005	127,366
2006	190,885

Fig. 5   Business segment at a glance
Source: Matsushita Corporation (2004, 2005, 2006).

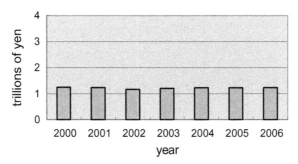

Year	Sales
2002	1,170,785
2003	1,197,481
2004	1,226,190
2005	1,229,768
2006	1,241,202

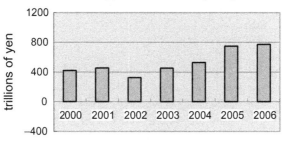

Year	Profit (Loss)
2002	32,611
2003	45,240
2004	52,759
2005	74,794
2006	77,135

Fig. 5   (*Continued*)

Devices • Sales

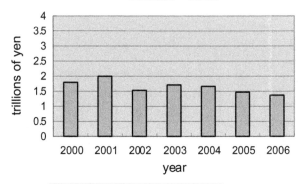

Year	Sales
2002	1,534,728
2003	1,709,732
2004	1,659,672
2005	1,469,007
2006	1,368,258

Devices • Profit (Loss)

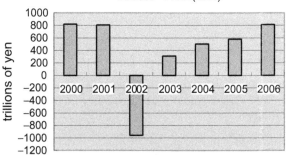

Year	Profit (Loss)
2002	(95,714)
2003	31,213
2004	50,099
2005	57,761
2006	81,111

Fig. 5 (*Continued*)

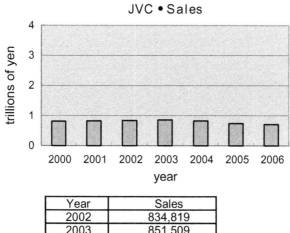

Year	Sales
2002	834,819
2003	851,509
2004	818,999
2005	730,209
2006	703,116

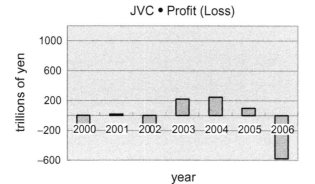

Year	Profit (Loss)
2002	(12,345)
2003	21,863
2004	24,675
2005	9,887
2006	(5,782)

Fig. 5 (*Continued*)

Others • Sales

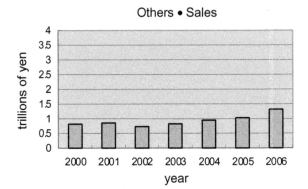

Year	Sales
2002	725,357
2003	819,055
2004	948,728
2005	1,027,123
2006	1,315,292

Others • Profit (Loss)

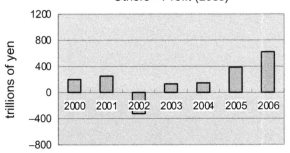

Year	Profit (Loss)
2002	(32,388)
2003	13,042
2004	14,701
2005	38,352
2006	62,225

Fig. 5   (*Continued*)

company has clear power to make decisions and execute them to achieve customer-based business development.

Furthermore, a capital governance mechanism was also constructed to increase the effectiveness of the restructuring. Specifically, the three fundamental items of the conventional autonomous division system — (1) the levy system, (2) the investment and dividend system, and (3) standards for business evaluation — were reconsidered.

Concerning the first item, the levies on each business domain company were previously variable, such as the funds paid to the head office in proportion to sales were changed to fixed payment according to the services provided by the head office. Concerning the second item, the basis for paying dividends to the head office was changed to a fixed percentage in accordance with the stockholding of each company, even when operating with a deficit. By doing so, elimination of deficit operation of the business domain company became a demand from capital, and expedited.

Furthermore, the overseas manufacturing companies are 100% funded by the head office or the regional corporate company (the organization that represents the head office in the region), and by each business domain company depositing 100% of the investment in the overseas companies below them in the head office, the funding and managerial responsibility business domain companies are substantially unified (under the autonomous division system, the ratio of investment, for the overseas business was 40% from the head office and 60% from the division). Concerning the third item, the criteria for the evaluation of business performance used by the head office were reduced to two indexes of performance that combine the capital market and vector, regarding the efficiency of autonomous responsibility and management and the transfer of authority. One criterion is CCM (capital cost

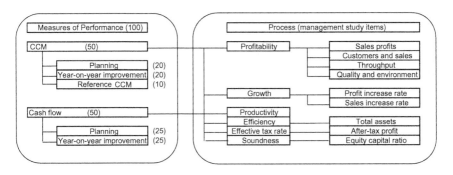

Fig. 6   Matsushita criteria for assessing performance

management), which represents the return on capital, and the other is cash flow, which represents the ability to generate capital (all on a consolidated global basis).

(In the autonomous division system, the profit on sales rate by product, profits, sales amount, and percent market share, inventory turnover rate,

Matsushita Electric Industries

Head Office Division	Management planning, accounting, personnel, general affairs and other such functional divisions, Management Quality Innovation Division, IT Innovation Division, Legal Affairs Division, Women Promotion Division, Corporate Communications Division, Environment Division, Product Quality Division, Materials Procurement Division, Intellectual Property Rights Division, the Tokyo Branch Office, Corporate Information Systems, Panasonic
R&D Divisions	Advanced Research Institute, Software Development Headquarters, Network Development Headquarters, Advanced Device Development Center, etc.
Marketing Divisions	Panasonic Marketing Headquarters, National Marketing Headquarters, Specialty Sales Promotion Headquarters, Electronic Materials Marketing Headquarters, Industry Marketing Headquarters
Overseas Divisions	North America Headquarters, Central and South America Headquarters, Europe Headquarters, CIS, Near and Middle-East Headquarters, Asia and Oceania Headquarters, China and Northeast Asia Headquarters, Overseas Business Headquarters, International Commerce Headquarters, Global Procurement Services, etc.

Wholly-Owned Subsidiaries and Business Divisions

Semiconductors
Panasonic AVC Networks
Panasonic Automotive Systems
Panasonic System Solutions
Home Appliance Group
Health Care
Lighting
Motors

[Independent Business Divisions] Precision Capacitor Division, etc.

Main Subsidiaries

Panasonic Communications (KK)
Matsushita Electronic Components (KK)
Panasonic Mobile Communications (KK)
Panasonic Factory Solutions (KK)
Matsushita Ecosystems (KK)
Matsushita Battery Industries (KK)
Matsushita-Kotobuki Electronics (KK)
Matsushita Industrial Information Systems (KK)
Matsushita Kogyo (KK) Victor Japan (KK)
Panahome (KK)

Fig. 7   Organization of Matsushita Electric

dcbt, and number of employees were emphasized). These criteria for the evaluation of business results are explained in Figure 6.

The CCM, an indicator of business performance that is expected to be positive in value, is calculated by the formula:

$$\text{CCM} = (\text{gross income} - \text{interest receipts} + \text{interest paid})$$
$$-\text{cost of invested capital,}$$

Cost of invested capital

$$= \text{assets} \times \text{percentage cost of invested capital (8.4\%)}.$$

The gross income is the operating income before taxes used in GAAP-based accounting rather than the operating income after taxes in the economic value added proposed by Stern Stewart & Co. Furthermore, the cost of capital can be considered as the minimum necessary profits that satisfy the expectations of the capital market, and is taken to be 8.4%. The asset balance is calculated in the following way:

$$\text{Asset balance} = \text{liquid assets other than bank deposits}$$
$$+ \text{fixed capital} + \text{investment.}$$

The emphasis on CCM and cash flow puts emphasis on reduction of assets and increase of profits and cash flow by the business domain company, and serves as a mechanism for expediting recovery from deficit operation and maintaining profitable operations.

In 2006, the organizational structure of Matsushita Electric was as shown in Figure 7 (Matsushita Electric website, 2007).

3 Administrations of Overseas Operations

In 2003, the situation of the Matsushita overseas companies is shown in Table 2.

Matsushita has positioned overseas business as the engine for overall company growth, business expansion, and the business tractor for the Group overall. On the opportunity of the Group restructuring toward the business domain structure system of 2003, each overseas business company was taken into the global consolidated management of its business domain company, and the CCM and cash flow of the consolidated global base were used to evaluate the performance. In addition, the corporations held by the regional corporate companies directly fund the Group companies in the

Table 2   Matsushita overseas companies (2003)

Overseas subsidiaries and related companies, 1 June 2003			
Number of companies by type of business		*Number of companies by region*	
Umbrella and support companies	5	North America	26
Manufacturing and Marketing companies	52	Central America	10
Manufacturing company	91	Europe	46
Marketing company	43	C S Middle East and Africa	6
R&D companies	16	Asia and Oceania	75
Financial companies	4	China and North Asia	63
Other	15	(Total of 41 countries and 226 companies)	

Source: Matsushita Corporation (2003).

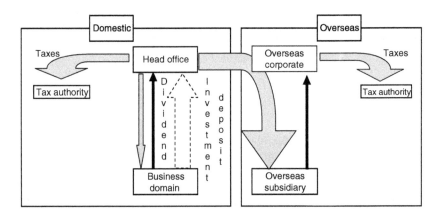

Fig. 8   Matsushita mechanism for global consolidated management
Source: *Weekly Diamond* (2003).

region and bear the responsibility for recovery of the funding. Through this restructuring, Matsushita expedited the consolidation of overseas business units and also achieved a turnaround of overseas business performance and improved the rate of return on investment (Matsushita Corporation, 2004). The mechanism for global consolidated management in Matsushita is shown in Figure 8.

The systems before and after restructuring, looking only at dividend and tax payments, are compared in Figure 9.

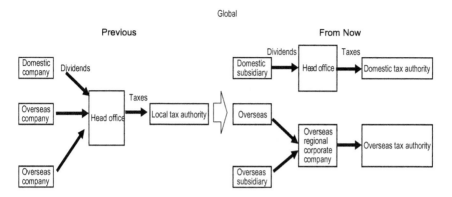

Fig. 9   Matsushita mechanism for payment of dividends and taxes
Source: *Weekly Diamond* (2004).

Concerning the management system for overseas businesses, the over-seas regional corporate companies represent the Global and Group head offices in their respective regions. In addition, all of the business compa-nies within the region are included in the global consolidated management of a business domain company, and at the same time are also included in the regional consolidated management of the regional corporate company of that region. In this way, the overseas businesses are managed from two aspects: the global strategy of the "business axis" of their respective busi-ness domain companies, and the growth strategy of the "region axis" of the regional corporate company. Matsushita conceives this overseas busi-ness management system as matrix management with the two aspects of "business" and "region" (Matsushita Corporation, 2004). This concept is illustrated in Figure 10.

The trends in sales in the various overseas regions of Matsushita are shown in Figure 11. This figure was created according to the divisions in the Annual Report, so it differs from the regional division by overseas companies as shown in Table 2. Please note that this comes from the year-to-year difference in the Annual Reports that we used for sources and that the divisions within Matsushita also differ.

Matsushita sales for the year ending in the third quarter of 2006 were 4.2829 trillion yen. Up to 2006, the total overseas sales had always been 100% or more compared to the previous year on a yen basis. The rea-son for this, as we also see from Table 2, is that although sales in North America weakened somewhat, there was a remarkable growth in the Asia

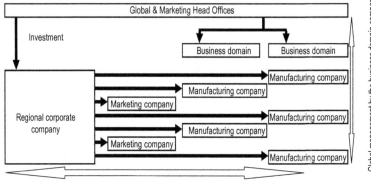

Fig. 10   Matsushita overseas business management system
Source: *Weekly Diamond* (2004).

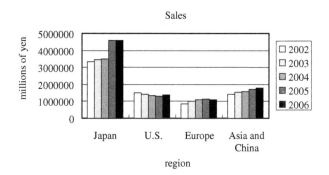

Fig. 11   Regional changes in Matsushita overseas sales
Source: Matsushita Corporation (2004).

and China regions. The decline in sales in North America was also unavoidable, considering the rise of the yen from 2002 (140 yen/dollar level) to 2005 (100 yen/dollar level).

Increased advertisement and publicity as part of the global sales strategy and brand development by unification to Panasonic as a global brand have been suggested as the reasons for this overall increase in sales (Matsushita Corporation, 2004). Since 2005, North American sales have continued to rise up to the present time, with contributions from favorable sales of plasma televisions. For the large-format TVs preferred by the North America market, plasma televisions are selected for their greatly lower price compared to liquid crystal TVs.

Comparison with the previous year on a local currency basis gives the result of 104%. Looking at this change in sales by region, it is 100% for North America, 102% for Europe, 103% for Asia excluding China, and 121% for China. The growth in China was particularly striking.

As the future strategy for growth in overseas business, the growth engine for Matsushita, the following five items had been set forth in the Leap Ahead 21 plan (Matsushita Corporation, 2004).

(1) *Produce overwhelmingly dominant products, focusing on V products*: To strengthen the introduction of V products that target the global market, shift the marketing functions of the business domain companies to the front line of the overseas market. Then, establish a product development cycle for the needs of individual markets and strengthen the simultaneous world-wide introduction and start-up of V products on the basis of an introduction plan that is finely tuned to the market.

(2) *Continue to strengthen brand power*: To strengthen continuing brand power, greatly augment investment in media advertising and aim for maximizing the effect of strong products and global marketing activities. By region, aggressively develop activities in Russia and other emerging markets in addition to China and Asia regions, in which particularly high growth is expected.

(3) *Promote restructuring and consolidation of business units*: Continue restructuring and business unit consolidation on the basis of a new management system. In particular, seek to optimize business expansion in China, which is steadily increasing in relative importance in the global economy, and in Southeast Asia, which is rising in importance as a site for strategic world manufacturing companies because of the trend of free trade agreements (FTA).

(4) *Achieve a business scale of one trillion yen in China*: To achieve a business scale of one trillion yen in China in 2005, the business domain company and Matsushita (China) work together to develop the emphasized product project toward strengthening product strength, and also strengthen the management system and promote restructuring of the distribution system.

(5) *Construction of a light and fast management system*: Concerning the overseas management system, aim to strengthen the responsibility

changes in the market by bringing into view major changes in, forms of distribution, such as goods distribution that does not go through the marketing company and Internet sales. In addition, incessant pursuit of efficiency through application of information technology to reduce operating costs and achieves an agile management system.

Looking at the most recent challenges to these five growth strategies, for example, for (1) producing overwhelmingly dominant products, focusing on V products, Matsushita believed that it was necessary to gain market share in a single effort. Then, as a condition for that sudden gain in market share, Matsushita considered simultaneous world-wide product introduction to be indispensable. One challenge to achieving simultaneous world-wide introduction was Matsushita's introduction of cell phone production at the first Kadoma factory (Kosuga *et al.*, 2006).

Furthermore, for (3), the development of business in Southeast Asia was optimized by reducing the number of production and sales offices. In January 2004, Matsushita expressed an intent to restructure the 73 production and sales offices in Southeast Asia at that time (11 in Singapore, 21 in Malaysia, 15 in Thailand, 10 in Indonesia, four in the Philippines, two in Vietnam, etc.) so that by 2006 there would be only about 44 (*Asian Market Review*, 2006).

Taking the development of the overseas cell phone business as an example, Matsushita had previously produced and sold what are referred to as 2.5-generation cell phones. As the devices became more popular around the world, however, the number of cell phone manufacturers also increased, resulting in severe price competition. For that reason, Matsushita realized the need to move to the production of cell phones for the third-generation communication system, for which technological development, complex manufacturing, and high costs were unavoidable (*Asian Market Review*, 2006).

At that time, Matsushita had cell phone manufacturing companies in the Philippines, Czechoslovakia, China and other locations, as well as the Shizuoka factory in Japan. In December 2005, the 2.5-generation cell phone business came to a gradual end, and it was decided to close the manufacturing companies in the Philippines and Czechoslovakia. Production at the China factory was shifted to third-generation terminals (Matsushita Electric Industrial Company website, 2007). Actually, the Philippines factory, Panasonic Mobile Communications Philippines (PMCP, established in December 1987, the former Philippines Matsushita Communications Industries) was liquidated in March 2006. The PMCP cell phone business began in 1999, and the total cell phone production was about 14 million units. It was expected to become an important manufacturing company. However, as a result of pursuing overall economy of scale for the Matsushita cell phone business, production in overseas manufacturing companies was consolidated to China. That move was probably also related to Matsushita's expectation of participating in the rapidly growing Chinese market of the time.

Furthermore, of the multiple cell phone R&D companies that were also located in China, the United Kingdom, the United States, and other countries, the facility in the United States was closed. The facility in the United Kingdom was chosen as the site for centralization of third-generation and later technology transfer and platform development (Matsushita Electric Industrial Company website, 2007). The fact that there was no particular restructuring of the multiple companies in China (Shanghai, Beijing, etc.) is probably for the same reason.

In the next section, we describe the relation of these manufacturing companies, R&D companies, and business offices to the head office, as well as the international management and accounting data.

4   International Management and Management Accounting Information

As we noted above, Matsushita had regional corporate companies, manufacturing companies, marketing companies, financial companies, and R&D companies as overseas subsidiaries in 2003. Matsushita also had five overseas head offices in North America, Europe, Middle and Near East, East Africa, Asia Pacific Rim, and China and North East Asia.

As overseas business operations, manufacturing companies cover production, marketing companies cover sales of products that are manufactured domestically or imported, financial companies cover funds and investments, and R&D companies cover production development according to customer needs in that area.

The two kinds of manufacturing companies include one-product companies that manufacture a single product and multi-product companies that manufacture multiple products. One-product companies are established by a business domain company and its profits are managed by the domain company; therefore, one-product companies are controlled by the domain company. On the other hand, multi-product companies are established by the headquarters in Japan at the beginning of expansion overseas. The regional corporate company manages these multi-product companies. Marketing companies are built and managed by the regional corporate companies. Financial companies and R&D companies are established and managed by the headquarters.

As we have already described, responsibility for investment, profit, risk management, brand management, etc., has been transferred from the head office in the area to the regional corporate companies. The regional corporate companies are taking on the previous responsibility of the headquarters. These corporate companies also handle business strategy in their region; therefore, these companies arrange marketing and manufacturing across several domains for business growth. These companies also take care of legal affairs, public relations, publicity, finance, and personnel management in their areas.

Under the divisional structure, each subsidiary was invested 40% from headquarters and 60% from its division. Subsidiaries in overseas used to pay a fixed percentage of sales to their division through the head office in their area as a consultant fee. The percentages were from 20% to 40% depending on the market growth, profitability, and the financial condition in each area. However, there were no distributions on the investment to the headquarters if the subsidiary was operating in the red. Subsidiaries could then operate their business with no distributions on the 40% of their capital from the headquarters (*Weekly Diamond*, 2003).

Under the present domain structure, on the other hand, regional corporate companies in principle invest 100% in the subsidiaries in their area, and the business domain companies deposit the same amount of money as the investment in headquarters. This connects capital and management directly. The subsidiaries pay distributions to their regional corporate company from their operation, and the corporate company pays taxes to the government. Other funds are pooled in the area overseas, which keeps the effective tariff at a low percentage. Business domain companies take all responsibility for investment and profit, and have to pay distributions with fixed percentage on their capital and surplus, even when operating at a loss. Domain companies have, therefore, become much more sensitive toward their profitability (*Weekly Diamond*, 2003).

Concerning management of overseas subsidiaries, marketing companies and multi-product companies are managed by regional corporate companies. One-product companies are managed by business domain companies. These companies submit their business plans calculated in local currency to a regional corporate company or a business domain company. The corporate company and domain company convert the business plans into Japanese yen and submit them to the headquarters.

The presidents of overseas subsidiaries operate businesses to achieve their approved business plans in local currency. Overseas subsidiaries do costing every month and compare the actual profit with the budget and the actual profit of the previous month. The result is reported to the corporate company or domain company. The performance evaluation is based on CCM and cash flow, because the headquarters evaluate its business domains on these two measures (Miyamoto and Kosuga, 2003).

Business domain companies are required to achieve their performance in a particular domain globally. It is a global structure based on business domains. On the other hand, regional corporate companies are required to achieve their performance on marketing (sales) and manufacturing in their area. It is a global structure based on region. Matsushita thus has two management structures in place at once. It refers to this dual structure as the "global matrix structure" (Miyamoto and Kosuga, 2003).

5 Summary

Matsushita Corporation was founded as Matsushita Electric Manufacturing Company in Osaka in 1918. Since then, Matsushita has been expanding with its clear credo and strategy. Matsushita had already regarded the overseas market as important in the 1930s, and had aggressively developed sales offices and factories in foreign countries. Moreover, Matsushita aimed for an overseas sales ratio of 50%. It can therefore be said that Matsushita is one of the most advanced global companies in Japan.

Matsushita expanded its business in the global market as well in Japan on the basis of a divisional structure, despite several organizational changes in its corporate history. After experiencing net losses in 2001, however, Matsushita changed its organization from the traditional divisional structure to the domain structure under president Nakamura. Matsushita has operated with 14 business domains since 1 January 2003. At the same time, the measures for performance evaluation were changed from general measures such as sales, profits, market share, turnover, debts, number of employees, and so on to only two measures, CCM and cash flow.

Matsushita considers overseas business to its engine for growth. It has put the overseas subsidiaries under global consolidated management by business domain companies and the subsidiaries are now evaluated by

CCM and cash flow. Moreover, the responsibility of investments and profits has transferred from the head offices in each area to regional corporate companies. This transfer means empowerment. Matsushita maximized its decision-making speed through this empowerment to adapt its business to drastic changes in the market.

With regard to organizational structure, Matsushita has put its overseas subsidiaries under both business domain companies and regional corporate companies; therefore, its overseas businesses have been managed with a matrix structure that is based on domains and areas.

This restructuring features (1) a flat organization, (2) selection and concentration of management resources, and (3) clarification of performance measures against the background of globalization and agility. These have become typical issues in recent years. We can thus learn much about international management and international management accounting from Matsushita's actual conditions in recent years.

References

Asian Market Review (2006). 15 January, pp. 36–37 (in Japanese).
Economist (2002). 18 June, p. 13 (in Japanese).
Kosuga, M., Asakura, Y. and Kimura, A. (2006). Process management of Matsushita Corporation, in *Strategic Process Management: Theory and Practice*, edited by Lee, G., Kosuga, M. and Nagasaka, Y., pp. 199–210 (in Japanese).
Matsushita Corporation (2002). Annual Report (in Japanese and English).
Matsushita Corporation (2003). Annual Report (in Japanese and English).
Matsushita Corporation (2004). Annual Report (in Japanese and English).
Matsushita Corporation (2005). Annual Report (in Japanese and English).
Matsushita Corporation (2006). Annual Report (in Japanese and English).
Matsushita's website (2007). http://panasonic.co.jp/ (in Japanese and English).
Miyamoto, K. (1992). Development of overseas businesses and management changes in Japanese companies: A case study of Matsushita Corporation, *Shogaku Kenkyu* 39(4), pp. 49–76 (in Japanese).
Miyamoto, K. (1997). Performance evaluation for overseas business in Matsushita Corporation, in *Theory of Global Management and Accounting*, edited by Yoshida, H. and Shiba, K., Zeimu Keiri Kyokai, pp. 160–181 (in Japanese).
Miyamoto, K. and Kosuga, M. (2003). Organizational design and management accounting for international management, in *A Study on Management Accounting for Corporate Value and Re-Organization: The Final Report*, Japan Accounting Association, pp. 243–260 (in Japanese).
Nikkei Business (2001). 28 May, pp. 26–51 (in Japanese).
Weekly Diamond (2001). 25 August, pp. 32–40 (in Japanese).
Weekly Diamond (2003). 8 March, pp. 27–47 (in Japanese).

Weekly Diamond (2004). 10 July, pp. 42–47 (in Japanese).
Weekly Toyo Keizai (2001). 26 May, pp. 26–59 (in Japanese).

Appreciation

In order to write this paper, we held extensive interviews on the management of Matsushita Corporation with Mr. Tetsuya Kawakami, a vice president, as well as Mr. Masayoshi Bandou, Mr. Minoru Uenoyama, Mr. Yuzuru Mizuno, and Mr. Yuuto Wakabayashi. We are grateful for their kind explanations, without which this paper could not have been written.

International Management Accounting in Sharp Corporation

Yoko Asakura

Associate Professor, Department of Economics and Finance
Faculty of Business, Osaka International University

Aiko Kageyama
MB, Graduate Student
Hiroshima University

Rieko Takahara
Associate Professor, School of Business Administration
Kinki University

1 Corporate Overview[1]

Sharp Corporation mainly consists of 47 consolidated subsidiary companies and 11 affiliated companies. The capital stock was 204,675 million yen as of 31 March 2007. The number of employees of the entire Sharp Group is around 56,800 (31,400 in Japan and 25,400 overseas).

Sharp divides its business into two main areas: production and sales of consumer/information products (audiovisual and communication equipment, home appliances, and information equipment) and electronic components (integrated circuits [ICs], liquid crystal displays [LCDs], and other electronic components). The two business areas are detailed in Figure 1.

1.1 *Company foundation*

A young man named Tokuji Hayakawa was awarded a patent for the "Tokubijo" snap buckle in 1912. He established a small metalworking shop in

---

[1]The contents of this section refer to the history of Sharp Corporation at the following website: http://sharp-world.com/corporate/info/his/h_company/index.html (accessed 2007).

Consumer/Information Products		
A/V Communication equipments	Home appliances	Information equipments
color television	refrigerators	personal computers
LCD color television	microwave ovens	POS system equipment
DVD players	air conditioners	LCD color monitors
LCD players	washing machines	PC software
MD players	vacuum cleaners	digital copier/printers
facsimiles	air pufflers, etc.	color inkjet printers, etc.
mobile phones, etc.		
Electronic Components		
LSI	LCD	Other electronic components
flash memory	TFT LCD display modules	solar cells
CCD and CMOS imagers	Duty LCD display modules	satelite broadcasting components
LSIs for LCDs	etc.	optical semiconductors
Analog Ics, etc.		hologram lasers, etc.

Fig. 1   Description of business[2]
Source: Sharp Corporation (2007). Description of Business (http://www.sharp.co.jp/corporate/info/outline/business/index.html).

Tokyo, going on to become the founder of Sharp Corporation, one of the world's largest manufacturers of consumer electronics products, information equipment, and electronic components.

The company started with three employees and initial capital of just under 50 yen (including a 40 yen loan). Mr. Hayakawa carried out research to manufacture a metal writing instrument, which at the time had not yet been developed. In 1915, he invented a mechanical pencil named the "Ever-Sharp Pencil" that took the world by storm. The name of the company today and its trademark are derived from this product. Following this success, Mr. Hayakawa continued to improve the product, and introduced one of the first assembly lines in Japan. By these, he was able to modernize the company and improve productivity.

In 1923, the Great Kanto Earthquake struck Tokyo and the surrounding area. Mr. Hayakawa's plant was severely damaged and was unable to rebuild the Ever-Sharp Pencil plant after the earthquake. However, with the help of his employees, he rebuilt his life and business in Osaka. Soon, in 1924, he resumed manufacturing metal writing instruments and established

---

[2]Sharp considers consumer/information products for end user as merchandise, and devices for their merchandise and other companies as components. In addition, they are given generic product name.

Hayakawa Metal Works in Nishitanabe, Osaka, where Sharp's head office now stands.

Radio sets were already in use overseas in 1924. In Japan, radio broadcasting was about to start but radio receivers had not yet been manufactured. Mr. Hayakawa recognized this valuable opportunity and decided to recover his position with a radio enterprise.

The next year, the company assembled the first Japanese crystal radio set. The sales of this radio set were quite good and the company became a pioneer of the new broadcast information age. In 1925, Mr. Hayakawa established the company's first sales base with the Utsubo office in Osaka.

In 1926, the company named its radio set the "Sharp Dyne". The company also opened a sales office in Tokyo, and began exporting radio parts to China, Southeast Asia, India, South America, and other areas.

In 1928, replacing the crystal radio set, new autodyne circuit (AC) vacuum tube radio sets were sold. As new products were developed, the company expanded its plants and improved production facilities. At that time in Japan, for many people Sharp was radio.

The radio sets and parts sold well in China. So Mr. Hayakawa concluded a distribution agreement with a major retailer in Hong Kong in 1931. He also began technological research that would later be used in television.

In 1933, Mr. Hayakawa visited Southeast Asia, opening new outlets throughout the region. And the same year in Osaka, construction started on the Hirano Plant, a new production facility for radio parts.

In 1935, Hayakawa Metal Works Institute Co. was incorporated with a capital of 300,000 yen. The following year, the company was renamed Hayakawa Metal Works Co. The company completed an in-house-designed intermittent belt conveyor system, which achieved mass production of high quality and efficiency.

Japan entered World War II in 1941. The company became the Army Aerial Headquarters factory and started production of military communications equipment. The company then established a short-wave and ultra-short-wave technical research laboratory for aerial radio equipment. The next year, the company changed its name to Hayakawa Electric Industry Co., Ltd., to reflect its change of focus.

World War II ended in 1945, leaving Japan in ruin. The company reduced its scale and concentrated on radio production.

In 1949, the demand for radio sets finally recovered, the business results of the company recovering somewhat, too. That year the company became listed for the first time on the Osaka Stock Exchange.

However, since there was shortage of food and materials, the occupation forces imposed strict fiscal measures (the Dodge Line) to control inflation. Consequently, the Japanese economy lapsed further into depression, radio manufacturers also being hard hit.

In 1950, the company was 4.65 million yen in debt. However, by desperate management efforts, the company avoided bankruptcy and began reconstruction.

Commercial radio stations opened one after another in 1951. The company released a new product, the super radio, and succeeded in the trial production of the first domestic television. And the next year, the company was the first in Japan to conclude a basic patent agreement with Radio Corporation of America (RCA) of the United States (US).

In 1953, the company produced Japan's first commercial television. One problem of mass production of television sets, at that time, was the difficulty in providing after-sales services. Therefore, the company continued pushing forward mass production and at the same time provided training for its engineers and dealers. Finally, the company had developed the perfect service system.

When the company began television production, televisions were too expensive for the average household and were mainly used in places where many people gathered. So the 17-inch model was the mainstream for public viewing. However, the company aimed to expand sales of the 14-inch screen model. Mass production of this model saw it become the standard television size. Demand continued, and product output reached a 60% share of the industry.

In 1954, the company built the new Tanabe Plant, which was equipped with the latest conveyor system in Osaka. This factory was able to perform the whole manufacturing process of television sets from wiring and assembly to packaging and warehousing using the latest endless conveyer system. This was a groundbreaking mass production factory for those days.

Japan's unprecedented economic expansion began in 1955. And the next year, the company constructed separate factories for electroplating and assembly of home electrical products at its Hirano Plant in Osaka.

The company also established a subsidiary, Sharp Electric Co., which performed mainly wholesaling to prepare for intensified sales promotion, and addressed the maintenance of the business base nationwide.

Moreover, the company began to establish a number of independent regional sales subsidiaries across Japan in 1958. The company started the

"Sharp Friend Shop System", whereby each store cooperated in marketing, promotion, advertising, and market development.

1.2 Becoming a full-range electronics manufacturer

The television boom reached a new peak in 1959. The company completed construction of a mass-production plant for home appliances in Yao, Osaka. The plant was capable of producing a broad range of home appliances at a single location, setting a precedent for the industry. Furthermore, the plant introduced modern facilities, which combined the creative power of the company and brought about the industry's first new product in sequence. The company accomplished a change to general household appliance manufacturers by the completion of the Yao Plant.

In 1960, the company completed construction of a plant in Yamato-Koriyama, Nara. The plant was a new base for production of television and radio parts, and would later become internationally known as the main production base of the company's electronic calculators.

The next year, the company established the Sharp Central Research Laboratories at the head office and aimed at new product development in the field of industrial and electronics-based equipment. This was the management's strategy of creating and fostering new core businesses following upon successes in the fields of televisions and home appliances.

In addition, the company had been paying more attention to the global market since the Ever-Sharp Pencil era, and laid emphasis on exporting.

After World War II, when transistor radios became commercialized, the company continued to export its products to the United States and other countries. Initially, the company's exports were handled by trading firms and buyers. However, it became necessary to establish a sales network within the company to provide quality after-sale services for local customers and stabilize sales expansion.

In 1962, the company established Sharp Electronics Corporation (SEC) in New York City. SEC was the first overseas sales subsidiary, started with 15 employees (including 6 Japanese) and capitalized of 150,000 US dollars. SEC focused on the sale of transistor radios and black and white televisions.

The company began establishing further bases overseas, actively developing markets in Europe and Southeast Asia. The transistor radio was already regularly used by people in 87 countries.

In addition, the company started solar power research in 1959 and succeeded in the mass production of solar cells in 1963. The development of the solar battery is the origin of the current company known as "Sharp Optoelectronics". In 1963, the company reorganized into three divisions, radio, home appliances, and industrial equipment, and established a service company, the predecessor of today's Sharp Engineering Corporation (SEC).

In 1964, the company developed the world's first all transistor-diode electronic desktop calculator. Research into developing smaller calculators by replacing transistors with ICs resulted in the creation of the world's first electronic calculator.

The company completed a number of specialized factories, such as for the production of radio transceivers in Hachihommatsu, Hiroshima, in 1967, and for the rapid growth in demand for color television sets in Yaita, Tochigi, in 1968.

The company established the first European subsidiary, Sharp Electronics (Europe) GmbH (SEEG) in Hamburg, former West Germany, to extend export to Europe. In 1969, the company established Sharp Electronics (UK) Ltd. (SUK) in Manchester, United Kingdom (UK), as the third major sales subsidiary next to the US and West Germany. In Japan, having adapted to the expansion of the electronic calculator market, the company established nine subsidiaries, including Tokyo Sharp Office Equipment Sales Co., Ltd. to sell office equipment.

In the same year, to raise new funds, the company issued 10 million shares of European depository receipts (EDR) for the first time, listing them on the Luxembourg Stock Exchange.

The company changed its name from Hayakawa Electric Industry Co., Ltd. to Sharp Corporation in 1970. This change synchronized the company name and trademark, marking the corporate direction from manufacturer of electric home appliances to manufacturer of electronics. The same year, the founder, President Hayakawa, was appointed as the chairman of Sharp Corporation, and Senior Executive Director Akira Saeki became the new president. With this new corporate structure, the company was ready to expand its role as a global company. This saw the establishment of Sharp Precision Machinery Co., Ltd., and completion of the national sales company system, which had been put back for several years.

In 1971, demand dropped and sales growth from customers coming into stores could no longer be sustained. To address this, the company formed "Attack Team of Market (ATOM)" teams. Each team was connected with a store and widened relations with customers by door-to-door sales to create demand. In addition, the company established Sharp do Brasil S.A.

Industria de Equipamentos Eletronicos (SDB), a joint production company in Manaus, Brazil, and Sharp Corporation of Australia Pty. Ltd. (SCA), a company established to market Sharp products in Sydney, Australia, to reinforce competitive power abroad. Furthermore, the company planned promotion of efficiency by centralization of management so that it could intensify market competition, and domestic sales companies could devote themselves to sales. Thus, 61 sales companies nationwide, except for Okinawa, were reorganized into 16 sales companies and 73 sales centers.

In 1973, the company succeeded in introducing a calculator with the world's first practical LCD unit. This electronic calculator was an epoch-making product. In the same year, Sharp's management creed of "Sincerity and Creativity" was born, being incorporated into management philosophy and basic policy.

In 1974, the company completed the new Tokyo branch office building in Ichigaya, Tokyo, as a base for new business activities in the metropolitan area. And the company established Sharp Electronics of Canada Ltd. (SECL). With this, sales companies were now established in five advanced countries: US, Canada, UK, West Germany, and Australia.

The company's output of electronic calculators reached 10 million units in 1975. In addition, SCA built a color television plant, starting operations in line with the advent of color television broadcasting in the country.

In 1977, the company implemented a product development system "Special Project Teams". The team consisted of cross-sectional members from different divisions and laboratories to tackle urgent problems, reporting directly to the company president. In this way, technologies from different divisions were streamlined into developing innovative products.

In addition, from the production side, the company succeeded in the world's first automation of the electronic calculator production process. Also the company consolidated its nine office equipment marketing companies into two main areas: east and west. The company strengthened the sales system of calculators, copiers, cash registers, etc., according to the product or market, and improved service to customers.

In 1979, the company established Sharp Manufacturing Company of America (SMCA) in Memphis, Tennessee. This was the company's first overseas manufacturing facility in the industrialized world that would soon produce color televisions and microwave ovens. In those days, Japanese trade friction worsened globally, and many Japanese companies reviewed their overseas plans. However, Sharp decided to focus on adapting products to the needs of the US market, together with a policy of contributing to the local community. This paid off, the company and its products being readily received.

In 1980, the company combined office equipment companies to form Sharp Business Co., Ltd. With its wide commercial domain, the company tried to rationalize the circulation of office equipment. The next year, the company completed a plant in Shinjo (Katsuragi), Nara. This plant produced solar power-related products, such as solar heat collectors, water heaters, and heat regeneration chambers, and started studying energy use technology.

In 1982, the company splintered off the credit section and established Sharp Finance Corporation to enter the consumer credit industry. And the next year, the company completed the Tokyo Research Laboratories in Kashiwa, Chiba, for research and development (R&D) of the latest technologies such as new media, very large-scale integration (VLSI) chips, and other electronic materials. That year, the company consolidated 10 service companies to form Sharp Engineering Corporation.

In 1985, to match the sense of values of diversified users, the company established the Life Software Center to research and to develop suitable software and products. This fact was the first organization of its kind in the industry targeting particular people, namely, "New Lifestyle" people, those born after 1954 who wanted products to match their individual personalities. So the company collected information on their lifestyle to identify their needs, and developed suitable products.

The company also established Sharp Manufacturing Company of UK (SUKM) in Wrexham, North Wales, as the manufacturing division of SUK; Sharp-Roxy Appliances Corporation (M) Sdn. Bhd. (SRAC), a joint manufacturing company; and Sharp-Roxy Sales & Service Company (M) Sdn. Bhd. (SRSSC), a joint sales company in Malaysia.

The following year, Sharp's president, Akira Saeki, was appointed as a chairman. Haruo Tsuji, then senior executive director, was selected as the new president. A new management team was established toward the 1990s.

The company established the Liquid Crystal Display Group and Liquid Crystal Display Laboratories within the Corporate Research and Development Group as one of its new strategies. The company believed that LCDs, which it had pioneered, would become a key electronic device, and focused on this as the company's main business for the 21st century.

In addition, the overseas bases expanded remarkably. For example, the company established Sharp Electronica Espana S.A. (SEES) as a manufacturing and sales base in Spain, and Sharp Electronics (Taiwan) Co., Ltd. (SET) as a manufacturing base in Taiwan.

In 1987, the company became famous for liquid crystal and created technology of the thin film transistor (TFT) LCD module. It was the best of its kind in the industry, and incorporated into color television attracted much attention.

However, the yen appreciated dramatically that year, and the Japanese economy declined rapidly. The company suffered, seeing a decrease in profits for the first time in 11 years, and began to reinforce domestic sales and shift production abroad. Consequently, the company reorganized domestic marketing companies to form Sharp Electronics Sales Corporation and Sharp System Products Co., Ltd.

In 1988, the company introduced a new personnel evaluation system in which employees set their own project goals, evaluating the results themselves with their superiors. This was a novel evaluation system that assisted in developing capabilities and increased motivation of individuals.

In 1990, the company established Sharp Techno System Co., Ltd. as well as Sharp Laboratories of Europe, Ltd. (SLE) as the first overseas research base in Oxford. The next year, the company completed a new liquid crystal factory in Tenri, Nara, and established an LCD mass production factory in the US. The company put together the Liquid Crystal Display Group and LCD Visual Systems Division, which had both started the previous year, and established a business system which included development, applications research, mass production, and marketing of liquid crystal.

In 1992, the company completed Makuhari Building in Chiba, a development base for multi-media and future information promotion. And a new building was also completed by SLE in the UK. This enabled the company to strengthen its global research and development for the 21st century. Moreover, the company reorganized two domestic sales companies, Sharp Electronics Sales Corporation and Sharp Live Electronics Corporation, to improve efficiency of regional business activities. Abroad, the company established Sharp Electronic Components (Taiwan) Corporation (SECT) as a sales base and color television plant in Taiwan. In China, the company established a joint manufacturing and sales company to produce air conditioners, Shanghai Sharp Air-Conditioning Systems Co., Ltd. (SSAC). This was the first production base for the company in China, operations commencing in 1994.

In 1993, production of both color televisions and microwave ovens at the US manufacturing base (SMCA) reached 20 million units. The company achieved a top share of the market for the supply of parts, a production system which emphasized quality, and for taking account of customer needs since operations began 14 years earlier.

1.3 *Toward the liquid crystal era (from the year 2004)*

In 1994, Sharp renamed one of its affiliate companies into Sharp Manufacturing Systems Corporation, aiming at its integration of the Factory Automation business. Furthermore, overseas, Sharp Shanghai Air Conditioning Systems Co., Ltd. (SSAC) completed construction of its new plants. After 1994, Sharp added rice cookers to its product lines and SSAC was renamed into Shanghai Sharp Electronics Co., Ltd. (SSEC). At almost the same time, Sharp Microelectronics Technology, Inc. (SMT) increased LCD production and Sharp Yasonta Indonesia (SYI) was established to produce color televisions and refrigerators.

In 1995, Sharp Electronic Components Co., Ltd. (SEC), a company for both manufacturing and sales of super-twisted nematic (STN) displays and LCD, was established, starting manufacture of middle and large format LCD panels for word processors and personal computers the following year.

In August 1995, Sharp established Sharp Semiconductor Indonesia (SSI), located in the state of Karawan, east of Jakarta, becoming the third base in Indonesia to manufacture semiconductors as ICs and optodevices. In November 1995, Sharp Manufacturing Company of UK (SUKM) obtained BS7750, the environmental management system standard of the British Standards Institute (BSI), the first Japanese company to do so.

In the US, Sharp established Sharp Laboratories of America, Inc. (SLA) for multimedia research in Camas, Washington in May 1995. With these new establishments, Sharp had developed a global triangle network including Japan, UK and US for the purpose of creating original products via multimedia technology, cooperating with the American excellent researchers.

In December 1995, Sharp established Sharp Electronics (Malaysia) Sdn. Bhd. (SEM) in the suburb of Kuala Lumpur to design and develop audiovisual products for Asia and supply parts for repair to Sharp's manufacturing bases and service centers worldwide. Sharp had succeeded in building its business all over the world as independent entities with independent R&D, manufacturing, and sales and service, focusing on local customer needs. So SEM has become the core base for product development in Asia.

In the US, Sharp also began joint research of the next generation videophone with AT&T and joint development of a MiniDisc (MD) data drive system with National Semiconductor Corporation. In January 1996, Sharp had begun the construction of a distribution center in the suburb of Los Angeles to strengthen its distribution function in western US. This center was also set up at the Los Angeles branch office of Sharp's US sales company (SEC) and in addition, Sharp Digital Information Products (SDI), its R&D core base, moved to this center and has become the largest base in this area.

In April 1996, Sharp established Nanjin Sharp Electronics Co., Ltd. (NSEC) in Nanjin, China, with Nanjin Panda Electronics Company Limited, the second largest electronics company in China, for the manufacture and sales of audiovisual products. This new company expanded not only into the air conditioner business but also into rice cookers, microwaves, refrigerators and washing machines, all major home appliances.

At this time, Sharp announced it would start joint R&D with Sony Corporation on large-screen flat displays using plasma-addressed liquid crystal (PALC) technology, which was a new method of discharging plasma to control liquid crystal elements.

In November 1997, Sharp announced establishment of Sharp Electronica Mexico S.A. de C.V. (SEMEX) in Rosarito, Mexico, to manufacture color televisions and other electronic products. The products as color TVs and vacuum machines manufactured in this factory were targeted to be sold in Mexico, North America, and other central and South American countries.

One month later, Sharp made another announcement that it would establish Sharp Middle East Free Zone Establishment (SMEF) in the free trade zone in Dubai, UAE, to strengthen its sales and service activities as a part of its strategy for rapid expansion in China, the Middle and Near East, Central and South America, and Central and Eastern Europe.

Additionally, in 1997, Sharp established Shanghai Sharp Mold and Manufacturing Systems Co., Ltd. (SSMC), a joint company with SVA (Group) Co., Ltd. of Shanghai, to manufacture and sell molds. Sharp also developed a 42-inch plasma-addressed liquid crystal (PALC) display in collaboration with Sony Corporation and Phillips Electronics N.V.

In June 1998, Mr. Katsuhiko Machida assumed the fourth presidency of Sharp and the period of integration of the business areas began. Under the new president's control, the company named itself "Crystal Clear Company" after "Liquid Crystal of Sharp", which had represented Sharp's major competitiveness, and aimed the whole groups' strength to be mobilized as "a one-and-only company that shines brightly in the international community" with originality in every aspect of its activities.

With this new aim, Sharp established two new companies, Sharp Document Systems Corporation (SDS), to strengthen its document business including copy machines, and Sharp Amenity Systems Corporation (SEMC), to expand environmental system business including solar power generation systems. Also, Sharp Electronics Sales Corporation and Sharp Live Electronics Corporation merged to become Sharp Electronics Marketing Cooperation (SEMC) to specialize and aggregate its sales system to take advantage of trends and strengthen the domestic sales frontline.

At the end of 1998, the company formed an alliance with Cadence Design Systems, Inc., California, US, and started joint R&D for large-scale integration (LSI) systems using Sharp's data driven media processor (DDMP) for the IT specialists in next generation. Further, Sharp announced its collaboration with NuvoMeEdia, Inc. for electronic publishing.

In March 1999, Sharp agreed to provide its advanced semiconductor manufacturing technology to 1st Silicon, an LSI manufacturer funded by the Sarawak State Government, US.

In May 1999, Sharp formed an alliance with Quanta to provide technology of thin film transistor (TFT) LCD. With this alliance, Sharp capitalized on Quanta's subsidiary company providing stable supply of the TFT Liquid Crystal, associated parts and PCs and contributing the manufacturing techniques.

In June 1999, Sharp formed an alliance with Conexant Systems, Inc. to develop process technology for $15\,\mu$m ultra high-density CMOS logic semiconductors for future digital home electronics and system SLI used for computer equipments, targeted to be ready by the fourth quarter of 2000. They also use each facility together for the development of LSI systems.

With the deregulation of import restrictions against Japan by Korea, which had been in place since 1978, Sharp established a sales company, Sharp Electronics Inc. of Korea (SEI), jointly with the Lee Group.

In Bangalore, India, Sharp established an R&D company to develop software for digital copiers and printers, Sharp Software Development India Pvt. Ltd. (SSDI). In 2000, Sharp established another company in India, Sharp Business Systems (India) Private Limited (SBI), jointly with Larsen & Toubro Limited, which enabled them to import and sell information products such as copiers and PCs and provide after-sales service in the Indian market.

In China, Sharp also established a sales company of electronic components, Sharp Microelectronics of China (Shanghai) Co., Ltd. (SMC), and in Europe, Sharp Electronics GmbH Poland Office (SEAP) was established as a sales base.

In 2001, Sharp established S.I. Solutions jointly with IBM Japan to provide an outsourcing service to Sharp Information Systems and implement ERP (Enterprise Resource Planning), a total information system to support product and sales management, and SCM (Supply Chain Management), a material procurement and inventory control system. Also Sharp had another joint business company, ELDis, Inc., with Tohoku Pioneer Corporation and Semiconductor Energy Laboratory Co., Ltd. to manufacture and sell TFT substrates for organic electroluminescent (EL) displays.

Subsequently, Kansai Recycling Systems Co., Ltd. was jointly established with Mitsubishi Material Cooperation. Also in Bracknell, UK, Sharp established Sharp Telecommunications of Europe, Ltd. (STE) as the R&D base for mobile phones.

In 2002, with the vision that all televisions sold in Japan should be switched to LCD models, Sharp built a plant in Kameyama, Mie Prefecture, to integrate its product lines for LC panels and large screens. In the Kameyama Plant, Sharp concentrates on developing and manufacturing LCD under the policy of "realizing the rich life with audiovisuals," accelerating the effectiveness of ideas, a fusion of "devices" and "products", by integrating its own technique for LC and television footage and developing new markets.

In 2003, Sharp signed an agreement with Germany's Loewe AG to cooperate in the development and supply of LCD televisions. Also in Mexico, SEMEX began to manufacture the "AQUAS" brand of LCD televisions, and in the US, SMCA began manufacturing solar energy modules.

In 2004, the Kameyama Plant started its full-scale operation from the large LC panels to large LC TVs called "Kameyama brand". By this time, Kameyama Plant had developed into an advanced facility with high-level footage technology with LC and environmental technology, becoming a plant representative of Japanese product engineering.

Sharp also agreed a joint development with the State of New Mexico, US, for photovoltaic generation as a new energy source.

In 2005, Sharp established Sharp Electronics Sales (China) Co., Ltd. (SESC). In addition, Sharp made an agreement to take over the LCD business of Fujitsu Ltd. and established a collaborative laboratory with Tokyo University on its Komaba Campus, named Todai-Sharp Laboratories.

Today, Sharp Corporation has two management creeds, "sincerity" and "creativity", to create prosperity for shareholders, customers, employees, and all collaborators. The company identified four strategies for mid-long-term planning, aiming to be a "valued one-of-a-kind enterprise" as follows (Sharp Corporation, 2007, Consolidated financial results for the year ended 31 March 2006, p. 7) (Figure 2).

(1) To build up its competitive leadership in the global market.
(2) To strengthen its commitment to global environmental protection.
(3) To strengthen its operating bases to support new models of product engineering.
(4) To evolve its organization to enhance its corporate competitiveness.

Sharp aimed to be valued as "one-of-a-kind Company" and implement "zero global warming impact" business on the environment globally, adopting its various strategies and tasks.

We have some data to show the scale of Sharp in certain indicators above and will describe each segment in Section 2.

2   Strategy and Organizational Structure

2.1   *Organization structure*

Sharp restructured in 2006, as shown in Figure 3, with the establishment of the new posts of corporate senior executive vice president for products business, corporate senior executive vice president for electronic components and device business, and corporate senior executive director for audiovisual systems and large LCD business.

Sharp also arranged five new presidencies of chief of general administration, electronic component and device business, information and communication systems business, environmental protection, and audiovisual systems and large LCD business. Moreover, Sharp set the general audit division as a part of building its internal control system.

As shown in Figure 3, Sharp introduced a business group structure comprising 11 business groups with 32 product divisions, each business group being regarded as an investment center under the internal equity system and each division being regarded as a profit center. Twelve staff groups and one

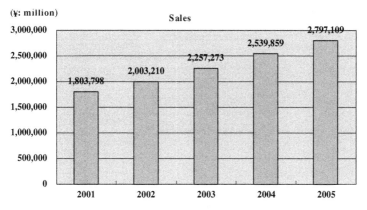

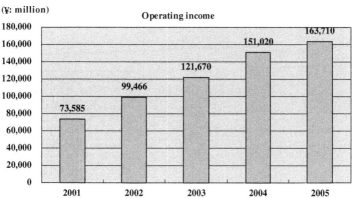

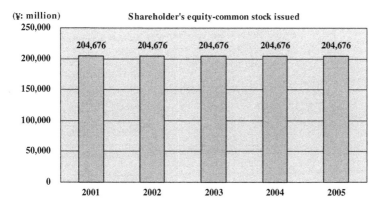

Fig. 2   Consolidated data of Sharp

Source: Sharp Corporation (2007). Consolidated Financial Highlights (http://sharp-world.com/corporate/ir/br/pdf/06all.pdf).

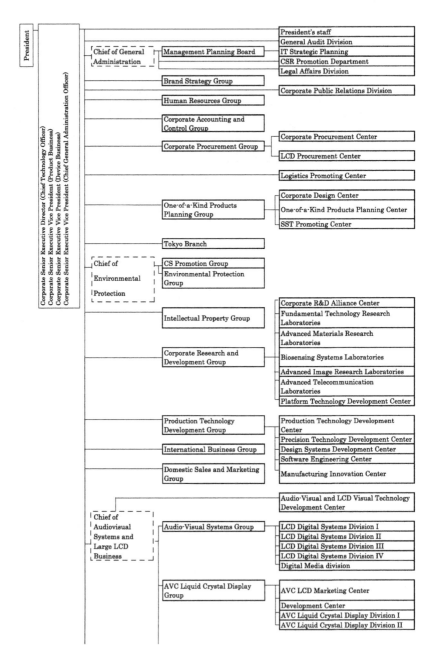

Fig. 3   Organization structure (as of 1 February 2007)

Source: Sharp Corporation (2007). Organization in Japan (http://sharp-world. com/corporate/info/ci/structure.pdf).

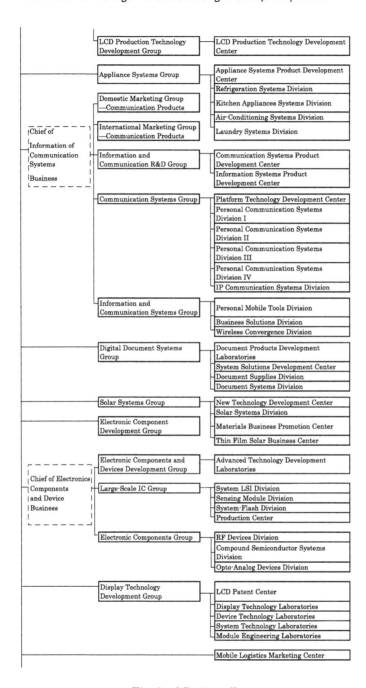

Fig. 3   (*Continued*)

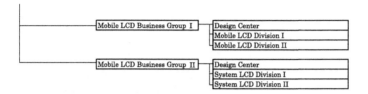

Fig. 3   (*Continued*)

planning group were also established, with the Tokyo branch office belonging directly to the head office. The Domestic Sales and Marketing Group and International Business Group control and manage the sales activities of products and associated parts as if they were a single business group. The former controls domestic sales activities and the latter, overseas sales activities. Most Sharp products are now manufactured at subsidiaries overseas. However, crucial product components are made in Japan to prevent loss of intellectual property.

At this point, we need to go back in time to explain one of the distinctive structures of the Sharp organization. In 1985, Sharp established Sharp Trading Corporation, as shown in Figure 4, which also indicates transactions between each company.

Apart from a few groups, each business group manufactures its products in one plant so as to be able to change its combination of products relatively easily and quickly to meet the needs of local customers. This system is a precursor of the Electronics Manufacturing Services (EMS), whereby each Sharp business group engages in designing, manufacturing, and customer services all in one plant.

With this integrated manufacturing system, Sharp began to manufacture LCD products from start to finish in the Kameyama Plant from January 2004. This plant has used the world's largest substrates ($1,500 \times 1,800$ mm) in its facilities and produced large LCD televisions with high image and sound quality. In this Kameyama Plant, Sharp rationalized its distribution, manufacturing, and assessment processes by the integrated manufacturing of large CL TVs and made this plant an epoch-making and vertically integrated facility (NIKKEI TELECOM 21, News Release Database, 18 January 2004).

Kameyama Plant No. 2 which began its operation introduced some techniques developed by FutureVision, a company established from 24 corporations. FutureVision has carried out national projects for the Ministry of Economy, Trade, and Industry. This Kameyama Plant No. 2 enables

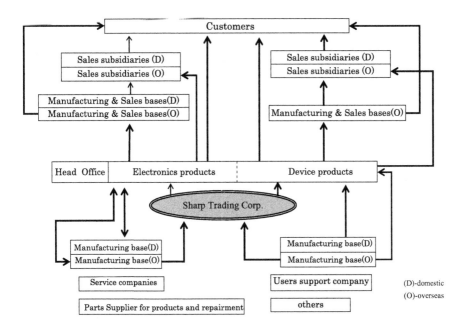

Fig. 4   Chart of the business in Sharp
Source: Sharp Corporation (2005). The 112th Annual Security Report (http://
www.sharp.co.jp/corporate/ir/library/security/112_yuho/index.html)   (in
Japanese).

Sharp to realize outstanding performance and cost-effectiveness in its sales
of large televisions, FutureVision being involved in the supply of materials
and equipment. Sharp has aimed to cluster its LCD plants to further take
advantage of cost reduction (*Nikkei Micro Device*, 2005, p. 148).

   In 2005, Sharp developed a new organizational framework in the audiovisual systems group which charges in manufacturing "AQUAS", as LCD
Digital Systems Division I, covering Japan and US; LCD Digital Systems
Division II, covering Asia; and LCD Digital Systems Division III, covering
Europe. This was the fruition of the idea to start business operations at
the same time in Japan, US and UK. Sharp also appointed division officers
specialized in each area of a division to ensure production and sales with
minimum delay (Terayama, 2005, p. 125).

   Sharp has focused on stabilization of the supply of panels by market
cultivation, strengthening its strategy for protection of intellectual assets,
prevention of outflow of techniques, and consolidation of safety and environment. With these visions, Sharp has established some business frameworks

to continue its investment as long as possible (*Nikkei Micro Device*, 2005, p. 148).

Some segmental data is shown in Figure 5.

2.2 *Management accounting*

Sharp introduced a divisional organizational system comprising two types of business units, manufacturing business units and sales business units. The manufacturing business activities and sales business activities are integrated and controlled vertically. Each business unit as a business group, division, sales company or manufacturing company is independently controlled and budgeted. Each makes mid-term plans of three years and implements short-term plans of one year with a rolling budget of every six months.

Sharp plans its whole budget in order as it is started from business units overseas to domestic divisions to business groups. Transactions among the business units are made by transfer pricing based on the market price and negotiation. Therefore, overseas business unit managers attend meetings at the head office in Japan to negotiate the budget and transfer prices for their business units. Next, each division collects cost and profit data from the manufacturing company overseas that manufacture the products of the division and prepares its estimated profit/loss statement. Also each business group collects the data of the divisions under its control and prepares its estimated balance sheet and profit/loss statement.

In the budgeting process, evaluations are carried out mainly using performance measures such as sales, operating income, the rate of cost, inventory, account receivable balance, and decrease in percentage of outdated products. In particular, performance measures of the achievement and of the percentage of completion for sales and operating income are the most important. From the year 2000, Sharp introduced an internal equity system in each business group and has evaluated the groups with a measure called "profit after capital cost" (PCC: Sharp's original performance measure similar to Economic Value Added (EVA)) subtracting capital cost as 5.5% from operating income after tax.

Additionally, Sharp has a unique strategic management control system called balanced scorecard personal (BSC-P) system, being the idea of a balanced scorecard to assess its business strategies and implement performance evaluations. With this system, Sharp can deploy company-wide strategies

(a) Consumer/Information Products

Fiscal Year	Sales (yen:million)
2001	1,276,078
2002	1,350,404
2003	1,442,702
2004	1,604,945
2005	1,740,773

Fiscal Year	Operating Income (yen:million)
2001	34,836
2002	43,646
2003	47,434
2004	57,035
2005	62,299

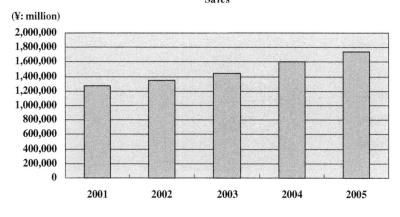

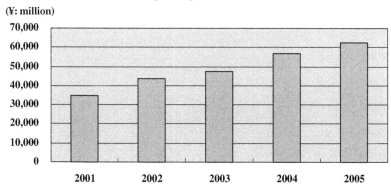

Fig. 5   Financial data of the segments
Source: Sharp Corporation (2007). Consolidated Financial Highlights (http://sharp-world.com/corporate/ir/br/pdf/06all.pdf).

(b) Electronic Components

Fiscal Year	Sales (yen:million)
2001	529,722
2002	656,810
2003	818,577
2004	938,922
2005	1,060,346

Fiscal Year	Operating Income (yen:million)
2001	37,269
2002	56,315
2003	73,971
2004	93,520
2005	101,914

Sales

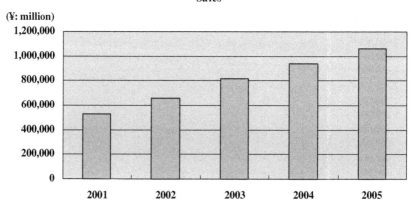

Operating Income

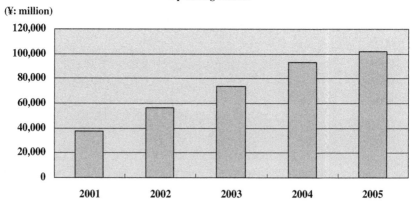

Fig. 5   (*Continued*)

over all operational levels (Sharp Corporation, 2004, p. 6). BSC-P promotes appropriate system operation in each term by delivering a message or warning along with the attainments of an individual's objectives on strategies. This system clarifies the linkage between the individuals' objectives and the upper level management's strategic objectives, namely, the interconnection of company-wide objectives among business groups, divisions, and individuals, thus enhancing the feasibility of strategies (Hayashi, 2005).

By establishing quantitative measures for performance evaluation, the plan-do-check-action (PDCA) cycle can ensure proper implementation of strategies. The change in performance attainment of strategies can be checked by computer (Hayashi, 2005), facilitating management and control.

Furthermore, Sharp controls the financing with profits and its funding for consolidated management with group funds. Moreover, Sharp has set its priority indicators for management as return on equity (ROE) and free cash flow, based on the profitability and efficiency of the funds, aiming to increase the value of all indicators.

In the case of free cash flow, even if it is negative, long-term fund management would recover the deficit within 3–5 years. Also it is important to observe how inventories are squeezed to secure efficient running costs and inventory costs even when free cash flow is positive in the short-term (Osada, 2004, p. 168).

PCC, mentioned previously, also promotes the recovery of the investments of each division (Sharp Corporation, 2007, Consolidated financial results for the year ended 31 March 2006, p. 5). For equipment, production cost is the 1:1 ratio of profit before tax and capital investments, and for devices, which may cost more than sales price, this ratio is 0.5:1, requiring continuous attention to funds (Osada, 2004, p. 169).

2.3   *Research and development*

Sharp's fundamental R&D focus is on one-of-a-kind products and devices, especially LCD applied products and solar cells, as well as on businesses that will drive future growth such as digital appliances and health and environment related products. In order to improve R&D efficiency and minimize R&D risk, we make the most of opportunities generated by industry–academic–government collaboration (Sharp Corporation, 2006, Annual Report 2006, p. 23). Sharp's R&D system is shown in Figure 6.

(a) R&D Bases in Japan (as of 1 April 2007)

Corporate Research and Development Group	Advanced Technology Research Laboratories Advanced Materials Research Laboratories Biosensing Systems Laboratories Advanced Image Research Laboratories Advanced Telecommunication Laboratory Platform Technology Development Center	6
Production Technology Development Group	Production Technology Development Center Precision Technology Development Center Design Systems Development Center Software Engineering Center Manufacturing Innovation Center	5
Audio-Visual and LCD Visual Technology Development Group	Platform Technology Development Center Digital Audio-Visual Development Center	2
LCD Production Technology	LCD Production Technology Development Center	1
Information and Communication R&D Group	Communication Systems Product Development Center Information Systems Product Development Center	2
Electronic Components and Devices Development Group		
Display Technology Development Group	Display Technology Laboratories Device Technology Laboratories System Technology Laboratories Module Engineering Laboratories	4
Division Laboratories	Development Center (AVC) Appliance Systems Product Development Center Platform Technology Development Center (Communication) Document Products Development Laboratories System Solutions Development Center (Document) New Technology Development Center (Solar) Advanced Technology Development Center (Mobile LCD)	7
Total		27

Source: Sharp Corporation (2007). R&D Bases in Japan (http://sharp-world.com/corporate/info/ci/r_d/index.html).

(b) Overseas R&D Bases

U.S.A.	Sharp Laboratories of America, Inc. (SLA)
U.K.	Sharp Laboratories of Europe, Ltd. (SLE)
	Sharp Telecommunications of Europe, Ltd. (STE)
Taiwan	Sharp Technology (Taiwan) Corporation (STT)
India	Sharp Software Development India Pvt. Ltd. (SSDI)

Source: Sharp Corporation (2007). Overseas R&D Bases (http://sharp-world.com/corporate/info/ci/g_r_d/index.html).

Fig. 6   R&D system

R&D structure in Sharp is made up of the Corporate Research and Development Group, Production Technology Development Group, Information and Communication R&D Group, Display Technology Development Group, Electronic Components and Devices Development Group, Audio–Visual and LCD Visual Technology Development Group, LCD Production Technology Development Group, development centers for a specific product in each group, the technical department in each division handling the design of the product, and project teams promoting the technology and product development across the organization. Thus, Sharp's R&D structure is a matrix (Sharp Corporation, 2006, The 113th Annual Security Report). The R&D expenditure is shown in Figure 7.

Furthermore, Sharp established overseas R&D bases including in the UK and US to facilitate the use of human resources in foreign countries and develop a product to meet the local infrastructure and needs. Sharp has also maintained close coordination and cooperative relations and effectively promoted R&D in advanced technology under a global R&D structure (Sharp Corporation, 2005, The 112th Annual Security Report).

Sharp has spent an enormous amount of money on R&D products, as shown in Figure 7. We will compare this percentage with the percentage in

	2001	2002	2003	2004	2005
R&D Expenditures (¥: millions)	144,744	152,145	162,991	175,558	185,240
Percentage vs. Net Sales	8.0%	7.6%	7.2%	6.9%	6.6%

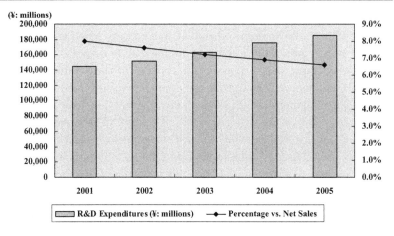

Fig. 7　R&D expenditures and percentage vs. net sales in Sharp
Source: Sharp Corporation (2007). R&D Expenditures (http://sharp-world.com/corporate/ir/br/pdf/06all.pdf).

	2001	2002	2003	2004	2005
Percentage vs. Net Sales	3.29%	3.06%	2.98%	3.11%	3.08%

Fig. 8   Percentage vs. net sales — Manufacture business
Source: Statistics Bureau in Ministry of Internal Affairs and Communications
(2007). Research Survey for Scientific Technique (http://www.stat.go.jp/data/
kagaku/2006/index.html) (in Japanese).

Figure 8 to see if the percentage vs. net sales in Sharp is high. Figure 8 shows
the percentage vs. net sales in enterprises except for public corporations,
financial enterprises, and insurance enterprises.

As a result, it turned out that Sharp's R&D expenditures vs. net sales
stood at the high level and they devote a lot of attention to R&D.

Sharp set up a distinctive R&D system, "Special Project Team", initiated in 1977. These teams treat products just short of commercial reality
and reduce the time required to take them to the market with competitive
advantage. The teams are flexible development units drawing together the
most appropriate people and skills from across the organization to bring
these products to market fruition (Nishi, 2007, p. 146). Members called to
work on the project teams are pulled from their regular jobs and devote
themselves to the project for a year to 18 months (*Nikkei Business*, 2004,
pp. 35–37). After completion of the project, the members disband and
return to their former posts.

Here is an example of how the Special Project Team concept operates.
First, the product or technology, previously judged as to whether it is a one-
of-a-kind or not, is presented in either top-down style or bottom-up style.
The main department selects members according to the product or technology. The main department has the freedom to requisition members from
any department. Furthermore, the team has a special budget for the project
over and above that of the original research budget. The progress of the
project is confirmed in the monthly integration technology meeting in which
such projects are initiated (Yanagihara and Okubo, 2004, pp. 114–122).

The leader used to wear a gold badge as well as board member in Sharp.
Now, the leader wears a name tag instead of a gold badge, although he or
she still has the same authority (Yanagihara and Okubo, 2004, pp. 114–
122). Ten teams are always operative at any one time.

Engineers are often familiar with each expertise, but most engineers
do not know anything but it. However, through their experience in a Special Project Team they can acquire more extensive knowledge and skills
(Katayama, 2003, p. 208).

The project teams have authority to obtain sufficient budget and poach talented people company-wide especially when the product or technology is particularly promising or revolutionary. R&D management in Sharp is referred to as "stock type" versus "flow style" (*Nikkei Information Strategy*, 2005, p. 245).

Stock-style management is to intensify effort and amass the precious managerial resources for the future. On the other hand, flow-style management is to concentrate on short-term revenue and the sacrifice of future profit. By operating stock-style management, Sharp has created a unique culture and intangible assets (*Nikkei Information Strategy*, 2005, p. 245).

The Special Project Teams are well-established in Sharp, and product development using this concept has become common at the divisional level. Moreover, Sharp establishes ways to further utilize the same Special Project Team according to the circumstances without any required letter of appointment to produce one-of-a-kind products or devices in a short time (*Nikkei Business*, 2004, p. 35).

Since 2003, Sharp has implemented an in-house suggestion system called "Sharp Dream Technology" (SDT) as a means to draw up new business ideas. While the Special Project Teams are required to achieve revenue in a short time, SDT is not held to such constraints to achieve results. Engineers tend to have a lot of ideas, but most do not proffer any as they tend to be too involved in their work. Consequently, by providing them an opportunity to share ideas, they can make a valuable contribution to discover new business ideas.

SDT can also serve to motivate employees who work on products or devices separate from the LCD core business. A new product corresponding to LCD derived from SDT is now in line for development (Nishi, 2007, p. 149).

2.4   *Environmental management*

In fiscal year 1999, Sharp first introduced environmental accounting to quantitatively assess the cost-benefit of its environmental sustainability management activities. The disclosure format complies with the Japanese Ministry of the Environment's "Environmental Accounting Guidelines 2005", in which environmental conservation costs are overhead costs, personnel expenses and investment associated with environmental conservation activities, including related depreciation costs (Sharp Corporation, 2006, Environmental and Social Report 2006, p. 29).

Both actual and estimated economic benefits are included in the disclosure. Actual benefit is economic effects directly assessed in monetary terms, such as cost saving from energy saving and recycled water, as well as profits on the sale of valuable resources. Second, estimated benefit is economic effects in equivalent monetary amounts, which cannot be cost directly, such as reduced greenhouse gas emissions and electricity savings from use of photovoltaic power generation and other energy-saving products (Sharp Corporation, 2006, Environmental and Social Report 2006, p. 29).

Also, Sharp refers to "Green Factories" as those factories that maintain a high level of environmental consciousness, determined by their unique set of evaluation, and assessment criteria. Sharp will plan to convert all manufacturing sites worldwide into Green Factories by fiscal year 2007 (Sharp Corporation, 2005, Annual Report 2005, p. 14).

Sharp aims to be a company with "zero global warming impact by 2010" (Sharp Corporation, 2006, Annual Report 2006, p. 21). Sharp raised the bar for environmental performance in fiscal year 2000, when it first included environmental criteria in its business group accomplishment evaluation system used semi-annually to evaluate all business group contributions to corporate management. In fiscal year 2004, Sharp focused on two important environmental criteria: the sales ratio of Green Products and Devices, and the progress rate of factors working toward the prevention of global warming. However, activities aimed at improving environmental performance at factories could not be accurately evaluated with these two existing criteria for judging business results. Hence, in fiscal year 2005, Sharp added two further criteria: how well accident prevention for environmental safety has been achieved, and how well the chemical substances risk reduction plan has been successfully implemented. Sharp will set forth precise environmental measures to help all business groups enhance their levels of environmental sustainability management and support the entire Sharp Group in achieving its objectives and environmental vision (Sharp Corporation, 2006, Environmental and Social Report 2006, p. 27).

3   International Strategy and Management Accounting

3.1 *Strategy and management of overseas business activities*

As of 2007, Sharp has 58 overseas companies and three representative offices in 25 countries/regions (see Figure 9).

Sales subsidiaries	27 companies in 22 countries/regions
Manufacturing bases	24 companies in 14 countries/regions
R&D bases	5 companies in 4 countries/regions
R&D company and parts supplier	1 company in 1 country/region
Finance company	1 company in 1 country/region
Representative offices	3 offices in 2 countries/regions
Total	58 companies and 3 representative offices in 25 countries/regions

Fig. 9   Overseas structure (as of 1 January 2007)
Source: Sharp Corporation (2007). Overseas Structure (http://sharp-world.com/ corporate/info/ci/g_organization/index.html).

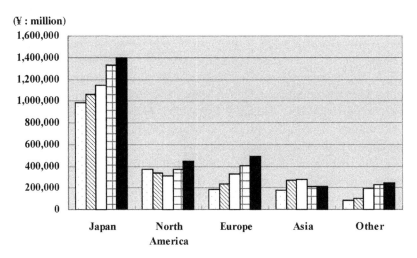

Fig. 10   Transition of regional sales
Source: Sharp Corporation (2007). Sales by Region (http://sharp-world.com/ corporate/ir/br/pdf/06all.pdf).

The recent transition of regional sales in Sharp is shown in Figure 10.

Sharp adopts a global productive divisional structure developed from a divisional organization. Each overseas manufacturing base produces products under multiple divisions at the headquarters in Japan, supported by each product division.

Sharp also adopts an international divisional structure for sales operation, overseas sales subsidiaries being integrated and managed under the International Business Group. Therefore, the structure of Sharp is a mixed global structure. Sharp has no regional headquarters as such. Representative overseas sales bases in each region — North America, Europe, China, and Asia — support the activities of the overseas subsidiaries in each region. The International Business Group based in Japan manages the international business activities of Sharp. The International Business Group makes important decisions on international business activities. The structure is shown in Figure 11.

Management in Sharp is very much home-country oriented. The International Business Group establishes, controls, and manages international sales, manufacturing and business bases, implementing company-wide strategies.

As above, Sharp has set itself the challenge for the future of securing competitive advantage, stably growing, and upgrading brand value in global market. Sharp has already strengthened sales of large LCD televisions to meet increasing global demand as the focus of its business in fiscal year 2006. Also, Sharp has established an optimum production system at the global level. Now, Sharp has consistently performed operations from packing liquid crystal panels to assembling LCD televisions in Japan, China, and Malaysia (Sharp Corporation, 2006, Annual Report 2006, p. 10).

Furthermore, to cope with the growing LCD television market in Europe, Sharp planned construction of a new LCD module plant in Poland in 2007, reflecting its desire to extend integrated LCD television production to Europe as well (Sharp Corporation, 2006, Annual Report 2006, p. 10). Sharp already has three bases for LCD television assembly in Europe. However, the new plant will enable the company to establish a system to provide LCD modules from within Europe to its Spanish plant and Loewe AG's

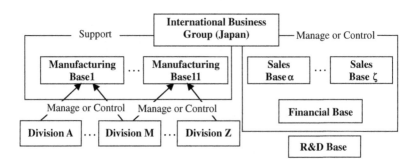

Fig. 11 International business activities and management control in Sharp

plant in Germany for production of large LCD televisions (*Nikkei Electronics*, 2006, p. 42). Sharp has three bases to assemble LCD TVs in Europe.

North America has been an export-oriented area for Sharp, with plans to construct a second plant in Mexico in 2007 to meet production for this market. The Mexico plant will enable reduction of transport costs and lead time, allowing flexible production to meet local demand trends and reduction of unnecessary stock (*Nikkei Newspaper Morning Edition*, 2006, p. 13).

Sharp will, furthermore, establish a system to produce LCD panels of a key device in the Kameyama plant in Japan, thus modularizing production of LCD televisions in the plants not only regionally, but worldwide based near the five major market (Sharp Corporation, 2006, The 113th Semiannual Report, p. 3). Consequently, Sharp will be able to sell LCD televisions to the world market in time, i.e., vertical integrated production (Tanaka, 2006, p. 29).

3.2 *Supply chain management*

Sharp has begun a full-scale process for introducing a supply chain management (SCM) system to share global manufacturing, sales, and inventory information. Sharp implemented this system to forecast demand for consumer/information products such as audio–visual equipment at each base. IT employees visited overseas bases to ask them to enter the exact production volume data into the system. Sharp has also introduced an in-house developed Global PSI Management System[3] (Figure 12) to consolidate information on manufacturing, sales, and inventory to reduce inventory.

The Global PSI Management System collects the orders and inventory information of products from the sales subsidiaries around the world. It also gathers the information on delivery schedules from manufacturing bases around the world, too. Divisions in headquarters decide which manufacturing bases are to produce products, when to produce, and how much to produce according to the information collected. In addition, employees in charge of sales can access the Global PSI Management System via a web browser on a computer and confirm delivery schedules at once. By using this system, the company aims to improve operating effectiveness at each base.

---

[3]PSI Production, Sales, and Inventory (*Nikkei Computer*, 2004, p. 16).

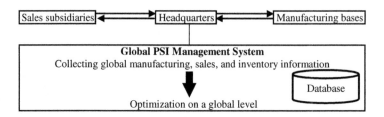

Fig. 12   Global PSI Management System
Source: *Nikkei Computer* (2004, p. 16).

However, introducing the Global PSI Management System to consolidate information could not realize optimization of inventory: it is also necessary to review the operation processes to coordinate production more immediately. Consequently, the company decided to implement a series of operation cycle for forecasting demand, designing sales plans, and preparing and reviewing production schedules weekly on a worldwide scale.

In January 2004, Sharp introduced the Global PSI Management System in the supply chain linking its manufacturing base in Thailand with its global sales bases keeping in mind regional circumstances and products. The manufacturing base in Thailand considers which base and which department participates in operations in advance. As a result, it could transfer most operations to a weekly cycle. Sharp subsequently introduced this system to its European region.

Sharp has now expanded the Global PSI Management System to 56 bases worldwide through a trial and error process. To ensure successful use of the system, it is necessary that sales bases and manufacturing bases understand the concept of total optimization of the supply chain. Therefore, Sharp has emphasized to manufacturing bases that "changing the operation cycle to weekly will strengthen the cooperation with sales bases. As a result, the manufacturing bases will increase production volume and improve performance" (*Nikkei Computer*, 2004, pp. 16–17).

3.3 *International management accounting*

As stated earlier, organization in Sharp adopts a global productive divisional structure developed from a divisional organization. Each overseas manufacturing subsidiary gets support from each manufacturing division as they make products for multiple divisions. Each overseas manufacturing subsidiary provides data on their own products to divisions that support each product. Consequently, each division collects data on their own products from the overseas manufacturing subsidiaries and prepares budgets.

Overseas business units perform all transfer transactions between overseas business units via Sharp Trading Company in Japan. In addition, financial management staffs at the Japan headquarters concentrate on financial management operations, including exchange risk control and financing. The methods include an exchange contract for debts and credits, a marry (offsetting foreign currency payable, including import with foreign currency received, including export), and a netting (offsetting debts with credits by focusing payment information between multiple companies in a specific organization).

These operations are performed around other parts of the world, too. The representative is Sharp International Finance (UK) PLC., an overseas financial company, performing financial management operations in the European region, namely long and short financing and fund management, exchange risk control, inter-company loans between subsidiaries and payment.

There are also methods for controlling exchange rate fluctuations. Sharp uses the planned rate as the exchange rate for budgeting in overseas business units. This planned rate is set by the Exchange Rate Steering Committee established in the accounting headquarters at the head office in Japan. Also, the company uses an internal rate as the exchange rate to measure performance. This internal rate is set four months in advance and used for three months. For example, the internal rate used from July to September is set at the end of March, and the internal rate used from October to December is set at the end of June.

The Exchange Rate Steering Committee uses the planned rate for budgeting and the internal rate for measuring performance. This means that the Exchange Rate Steering Committee assures the anticipated rate. Thus, divisional managers are not responsible for the effects of exchange rate fluctuations.

Therefore, management of exchange rate risk is performed from the position of the whole company at the accounting headquarter of the home office. The accounting headquarters acts as if it were a bank within a company so business unit managers can deal with future income and expenditure using the internal rate. Business unit managers both make decisions to accomplish goals and are evaluated using the internal rate. Moreover, they can accomplish the full enterprise goal by achieving a given goal, leading to goal congruence of the whole company.

Performance in overseas business units is evaluated by comparing budget in local currency with performance in local currency. Further, the performance in divisions is converted at the internal rate because performance evaluation in divisions includes yen equivalents in overseas business unit. Thus, it is obvious not to give divisional manager the responsibility for exchange rate fluctuations.

References

Hayashi, M. (2005). Sharp concatenate organization's strategy target of balanced-scorecard, change it to personal target and realize to execute a strategy, Conference Presentation in the Japanese Association of Management Accounting (in Japanese).

Katayama, O. (2003). Reviving white goods to growth products: Desperate efforts to produce key devices representative as market leaders of liquid-crystal technology, *Voice*, January, pp. 202–211 (in Japanese).

Nikkei Business (2004). Enterprises to continue to make a big hit to Sharp Corporation — Concentration power to focus breakthrough, No. 1271, 13 December, pp. 35–37 (in Japanese).

Nikkei Computer (2004). Introduction of SCM in Sharp to final stage-sharing production, sales, and inventory information in 56 bases worldwide, No. 613, 15 November, pp. 16–17 (in Japanese).

Nikkei Electronics (2006). Sharp to construct module factory in Poland, 24 April, pp. 42–43 (in Japanese).

Nikkei Information Strategy (2005). Stock-style management in Sharp, No. 153, January, p. 245 (in Japanese).

Nikkei Micro Device (2005). Sharp fuses development strength and production strength to compete on vertical integrating force, December, p. 148 (in Japanese).

Nikkei Newspaper Morning Edition (2006). LCD TV's base in Mexico: Sharp to rapidly supply North America, 30 August, p. 13 (in Japanese).

Nishi, T. (2007). Expanding the target of CFT lasting up to thirty years made possible by building a resource recycle structure-carried out by management! Project Management Sharp, *Nikkei Information Strategy* (179), pp. 146–149 (in Japanese).

Osada, T. (2004). *The Secret of Sharp: The Power in Japanese Enterprises to Keeping on Winning*, President Co. (in Japanese).

Sharp Corporation (2004). Annual Report 2004.

Sharp Corporation (2005). Annual Report 2005.

Sharp Corporation (2005). The 112th Annual Security Report (http://www.sharp.co.jp/corporate/ir/library/security/112_yuho/index.html) (in Japanese).

Sharp Corporation (2006). Annual Report 2006.

Sharp Corporation (2006). Environmental and Social Report 2006.

Sharp Corporation (2006). The 113th Annual Security Report (http://www.
    sharp.co.jp/corporate/ir/other/113_yuho/index.html) (in Japanese).
Sharp Corporation (2006). The 113th Semiannual Report (http://www.
    sharp.co.jp/corporate/ir/other/113_hanki/index.html) (in Japanese).
Sharp Corporation (2007). Consolidated Financial Highlights (http://sharp-
    world.com/corporate/ir/br/pdf/06all.pdf).
Sharp Corporation (2007). Consolidated financial results for the year ended
    31 March 2006 (http://www.sharp.co.jp/corporate/ir/library/financial/pdf/
    2006/1/all.pdf) (in Japanese).
Sharp Corporation (2007). Description of Business (http://www.sharp.co.jp/
    corporate/info/outline/business/index.html).
Sharp Corporation (2007). Organization in Japan (http://sharp-world.com/
    corporate/info/ci/structure.pdf).
Sharp Corporation (2007). Overseas R&D Bases (http://sharp-world.com/
    corporate/info/ci/g_r_d/index.html).
Sharp Corporation (2007). Overseas Structure (http://sharp-world.com/
    corporate/info/ci/g_organization/index.html).
Sharp Corporation (2007). R&D Bases in Japan (http://sharp-world.com/
    corporate/info/ci/r_d/index.html).
Sharp Corporation (2007). R&D Expenditures (http://sharp-world.com/
    corporate/ir/br/pdf/06all.pdf).
Sharp Corporation (2007). Sales by Region (http://sharp-world.com/corporate/
    ir/br/pdf/06all.pdf).
Sharp Corporation (2007). Sharp History (http://sharp-world.com/corporate/
    info/his/h_company/index.html).
Statistics Bureau in Ministry of Internal Affairs and Communications (2007).
    Research Survey for Scientific Technique (http://www.stat.go.jp/data/
    kagaku/2006/index.html) (in Japanese).
Tanaka, N. (2006). LCD TV to the world: Winning by competitiveness, *Nikkei
    Micro Device*, June, pp. 28–29 (in Japanese).
Terayama, S. (2005). Hope for big-name brand in the world, *Nikkei Business*, 18
    July, pp. 122–125 (in Japanese).
Yanagihara, K. and Okubo, T. (2004). *Stock Style's Management in Sharp*,
    Diamond Co. (in Japanese).

Additional Statement

This paper is based on interviews carried out over five hours at Sharp's
headquarters (22–22, Nagaike-cho, Abeno-ku, Osaka 545–8522, Japan)
on 9 August 2002, together with more up-to-date information from
the corporation's website. Members from Sharp attending the interview
were general group managers of the Corporate Accounting and Control
Group, Mr. Tetsuo Onishi, Mr. Kiyokazu Kawabe, Mr. Chiaki Komaru,
Mr. Satoshi Sakakibara, Mr. Tadashi Sakamoto, Mr. Shoji Kobayashi,

Mr. Yujiro Nishio, and Mr. Manabu Morita. There were a further 18 inter-viewers from the International Management Accounting Committee. The object of this survey was to gain an understanding of the actual situa-tion of international management accounting in Sharp. The main questions focused on were: (1) general information; (2) preparation of financial state-ments; (3) performance evaluation criteria; (4) bases for measuring financial performance measurements; (5) environmental problems complicating per-formance evaluation of overseas business units; (6) formulation of strategies; and (7) intellectual assets.

International Management Accounting for SANYO Electric Co., Ltd.

Keisuke Sakate
Osaka University of Commerce

Masafumi Tomita
Certified Public Accountant (Japan)

1 Introduction of SANYO Electric Co., Ltd.

1.1 *The establishment and management policy of SANYO Electric Co., Ltd.*

SANYO Electric Co., Ltd. (hereafter SANYO) began as a small workshop named SANYO Electric Works, which was founded at Moriguchi City, Osaka Prefecture, in 1947 by Toshio Iue from Awajishima Island. Toshio wanted to conduct business on a small scale and be involved with the production process so that he could concentrate solely on developing quality products. He felt that doing business in this way would keep his employees happy, and he would finally be able to contribute to society.

Prior to World War II, Toshio Iue worked for Matsushita Electric Industry Co., Ltd. (hereafter Matsushita Electric Industry), and played an active part as the right-hand man to his brother-in-law, Konosuke Matsushita. Konosuke was the founder of Matsushita Electric Industry and was married to Toshio's sister. However, after the war, the General Headquarters of Allied Forces (GHQ) decided it was necessary to penalize companies that had supported Japan's military effort by producing munitions. For Matsushita Electric Industry, that penalty involved the removal of one executive officer. Toshio decided that he should be the one to leave and founded SANYO Electric Works.

The name SANYO means *three oceans*, referring to the Pacific, Atlantic, and Indian Oceans. The founder's goal was to bring his technology and services across these three oceans, to the whole world. The introduction of this name defined the target and policy of the business. Additionally, the creation of the word SANYO was thought to be emotionally driven by the founder, who had wanted to work with the whole world.

"Quality work to be proud of, the world over" is SANYO's "Principle of Conduct". SANYO seeks to develop unique technologies and offer excellent products and sincere services that will be loved and trusted by people around the world. This objective is defined in SANYO's management philosophy: "We are committed to becoming an indispensable element in the lives of people all over the world." The company's long-term vision is as follows:

(1) Be an excellent company, which features global management and high performance.
(2) Be one of the best manufacturers of electronics that employ progressive technology.
(3) Be a company that contributes to society.
(4) Be a company that is trusted by consumers because of excellent marketing.
(5) Be a company that is staffed by aggressive, vigorous employees.

SANYO has reported their environmental and social activities every year as Sustainability Report. Their first Environmental Report was released in June 2006. They tried to improve employees' environmental awareness by creating the Solar Ark, a symbol of clean energy, constructed in 2002 at the Gifu plant. The company works actively to disclose information to consumer about its activities to help spread the environmental message to the whole world.

The principal business of SANYO is classified by the segment information into four groups: the Consumer Group, including AV equipment, communication equipment, and home appliance products; the Commercial Group, including industrial electric products (e.g., refrigerators) and industrial equipment; the Component Group, including electronic devices and batteries; and the Other Group, including financials, logistics, maintenance, and information services. Previously, SANYO had six groups: AV equipment, information equipment, electric equipment, industrial equipment, electronic devices, and batteries and others. However, since March 2005, SANYO has changed their segmentation from six groups to four groups, based on the product's nature and market similarity. The belief is that this will create greater consistency in the internal management system and lead to more accountability in the disclosure information. By this change in segmentation, the classifying of the segment information was harmonized with the classifying of the company group system beginning in SANYO's 2003 fiscal year. The main business area of each segment is described in detail in Table 2.

1.2 History of SANYO's overseas transactions

It was the founder's philosophy that "We are committed to becoming an indispensable element in the lives of people all over the world." SANYO began doing business in the global market very early in their company's history.

Founded in 1947, SANYO soon developed, manufactured, and sold the dynamo-powered bicycle lamp, which experienced excellent growth and received positive reviews in the market. In 1949, GHQ requested 5000 bicycle lamps to export overseas, and so SANYO experienced their first foray into the global market. SANYO's export business soon grew, developing mainly in the Southeast Asian market, and SANYO Electric Co., Ltd. was officially incorporated in 1950. SANYO was listed on the Tokyo Stock Exchange and the Osaka Stock Exchange in 1954 to continue their financial growth. Once SANYO was incorporated, they began to actively manufacture and sell home appliances, such as radios and washing machines called "home appliance." SANYO's achievement in the manufacturing and sales of washing machines in the fifties was the first step toward branching out into manufacturing a wide variety of appliances. Even though SANYO suffered some sizeable losses from a bitter fight between their management and the labor union, their sales reached 14 billion yen and they employed approximately 8,000 people in the fiscal period ending May 1959 (in those days, fiscal periods were six months long).

During the 1950s, SANYO's overseas transaction built on solid growth and the company expanded the market to the Middle East and Latin America. The Overseas Sector, which handled overseas transactions, changed its name to Trading Division in 1956. In addition, SANYO aligned with Channel Master (a division of PCT International Inc.) in the United States in 1958. SANYO began manufacturing transistor radios, becoming the original equipment manufacturer (OEM).

In the 1960s, SANYO expanded their domestic production bases in Gunma, Awaji Island, and Tottori. In 1960, SANYO established SANYO Electric (Hong Kong) Ltd., which became their first overseas manufacturing subsidiary in Hong Kong. In the same year, SANYO Trading Co., Ltd., which would later be reorganized as SANYO Sales & Marketing Corporation, was established. SANYO was now a full-fledged global business.

1.3   *SANYO's breakthrough and their business activity in the global market*

SANYO's full-fledged global business really began in the 1960s. In 1960, SANYO established SANYO Electric (Hong Kong) Ltd., which was their first overseas manufacturing subsidiary, and then they established a sales subsidiary in America, named SANYO Electric Inc. in 1961. Additionally, in 1962, they established a sales subsidiary in Malaysia and aggressively began doing business globally. With their new manufacturing subsidiaries, SANYO became established in numerous countries, such as Taiwan, Ghana, Spain, Singapore, and Malaysia, in only a few years. After that, they established subsidiaries in Thailand, England, and Korea. Within 10 years, they established approximately 10 subsidiaries. Many companies established during that time took the important role of being an overseas foothold for SANYO.

In the 1970s, the movement to establish manufacturing subsidiaries was accelerated. SANYO established a manufacturing subsidiary in Indonesia in 1970 and aggressively established new sales or manufacturing subsidiaries in areas where they did not yet have business bases — for example, Vietnam, the Philippines, Kenya, Australia, and Germany — or where they had already set up several business bases — for example, Singapore, Hong Kong, Taiwan, and Korea — and expanded their business areas. In this time, the core businesses of SANYO, such as semiconductors, experienced massive growth. Therefore, almost all subsidiaries established during this periods manufactured semiconductors or other electronic devices.

SANYO actively began overseas financing at this time. For example, SANYO issued their first Curaso Depositary Receipts (CDR; they are the depositary receipts that are issued in Curaso) in the European market in October 1969, and 20 million dollars in their first bonds in the European and Arabic markets in 1975. This transaction is designed to promote the circulation of a foreign company's stocks in the overseas market. The securities company that is left in trust with the stocks promotes the circulation by securitization and selling it. SANYO discloses the consolidated financial statement by SEC basis, starting with this issuing. In 1977, they listed unsponsored American Depositary Receipts (ADR) on the National Association of Securities Dealers Automated Quotations (NASDAQ). This action was linked to the movement of listings in the overseas market for SANYO.

In the 1980s, the movement to establish new bases was accelerated. SANYO set up new bases around the world, in countries such as Argentina, India, England, Mexico, Canada, China, and Germany. Under their policy of owning 100 manufacturing plants worldwide, they established approximately 30 overseas subsidiaries, both sales and manufacturing, during this decade.

Not only did SANYO set up their sales and manufacturing base, but they also took care of global group management, managing their overseas subsidiaries and using assets more efficiently during the 1980s. For example, group reorganization for merged sales subsidiaries and the establishment of the SANYO North America Corporation helped them gain regional control.

SANYO was listed on the Swiss stock market in June 1981 and on the Paris Bourse in November 1985. SANYO was also listed on the global stock market of Amsterdam and Frankfurt, in addition to NASDAQ, which enabled financing from global markets. SANYO delisted their stock from the stock market of Amsterdam on 31 March 2007, the Swiss stock market on 31 May 2007 and the Paris Bourse on 28 June 2007. Finally, they delisted from NASDAQ on 28 November 2007. Now, SANYO is only listed on the domestic market (Tokyo Stock Exchange and Osaka Securities Exchange).

In the 1990s, SANYO's overseas operations were changing to aggressively advance into China. In 1992, SANYO established their first subsidiary in China, named Dalian SANYO Refrigeration Co., Ltd., which manufactured large adsorption-freezers. Around Dalian, they established their new bases in China, which included Shenyang, Shenzen, and Suzhou. As a result, they established over 15 manufacturing subsidiaries in China during the nineties. In addition, SANYO also took care of the management structure by establishing new subsidiaries to control the region. SANYO Electric (China) Co., Ltd. was established in 1995 in Beijing, and the other new subsidiary, which controlled AV business in China, was created in Guangzhou in 1996.

SANYO continued to consistently and aggressively establish themselves overseas, not only in European countries, such as Portugal, Italy, and the Netherlands, but also in Indonesia, Mexico, and South Africa. They were not specific about the target countries and areas.

Beginning in the mid-1980s, SANYO began to actively contract international business alliances focused on semiconductors and batteries with some of the largest companies in the world, including Ford Motor Company, General Electric Company, IBM Corporation, and Eastman Kodak Company. After 2000, the scope of these business alliances was expanded. In 2002, SANYO targeted expanding markets in China and established a comprehensive business alliance and sales and manufacturing partnership with Haier Group, the largest home appliance manufacturers in China. In the same year, they established a relationship with the Samsung Advanced Institute of Technology, focused on generic technology, and they have established business alliance actively with SANYO's competitor.

1.4 *Present-day SANYO*

The SANYO Group consists of 309 companies, including 236 consolidated subsidiaries and 73 related companies that are added to SANYO under the equity method (102 domestic subsidiaries, 43 domestic related companies, 134 overseas subsidiaries, and 30 overseas related companies). As of 31 March 2006, their capital was 322,242 million yen and the numbers of employees were 106,389.

Figures 1 and 2 show that in the fiscal year ending 31 March 2004, SANYO achieved their best performances in revenues and profits. (The numerical value of the description from Figures 1 to 6 reflects the restatements under US-GAAP.)

The deterioration of profitability in the fiscal year ending 31 March 2005, recorded 171,500 million yen in consolidated net losses, because a semiconductor wafer-process manufacturing subsidiary named Niigata SANYO Electric Co., Ltd. (currently, SANYO Semiconductor Manufacturing Co., Ltd.) was hit by the earthquake in Niigata-ken Chuetsu on October 2004 and recorded extraordinary losses in that fiscal year. However, the number

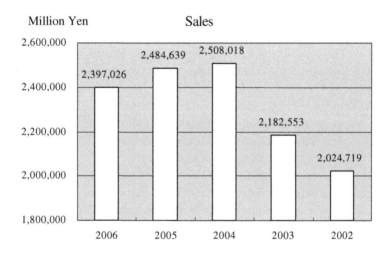

Fig. 1   Changes in sales

Source: SANYO (2006a).

Million Yen   Operating Income (Loss)

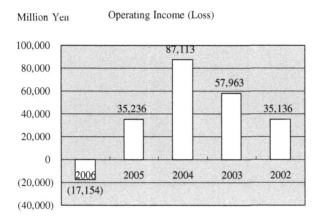

Fig. 2   Changes in operating income (loss)
Source: SANYO (2006a).

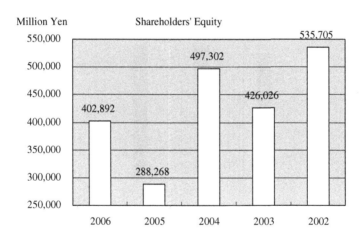

Fig. 3   Changes in shareholders' equity of SANYO
Source: SANYO (2006a).

of employees during this depression increased because SANYO expanded
the scope of consolidation and increased the number of subsidiaries.

On 1 April 2003, SANYO underwent fundamental reforms, setting up
the business group system and the business unit system in their operation system and in managerial organization. These measures would be used
to overcome a crisis in the fiscal year of 2005, when they recorded huge
amount of losses. Tomoyo Nonaka, a former journalist, was brought in as

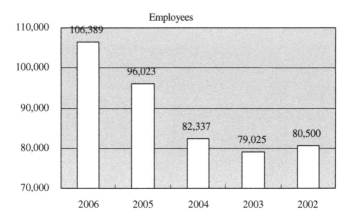

Fig. 4   Changes in number of employees
Source: SANYO (2006a).

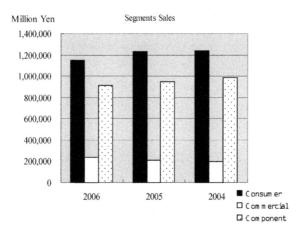

Fig. 5   Changes in segment sales
Source: SANYO (2006a).

the new CEO, and she reorganized the board of directors. She set the new company's vision with the slogan "Think GAIA", and started the "SANYO EVOLUTION PROJECT." This revised business model led to the development and implementation of three new business plans: the Business Portfolio Evolution Plan, for business portfolio reforms; the Corporate DNA Evolution Plan, for corporate culture, organization, and management process reforms; and the Financial Evolution Plan, for improving SANYO's financial standing. (The description about this section referred to the website of SANYO.)

Million Yen   Regional Sales

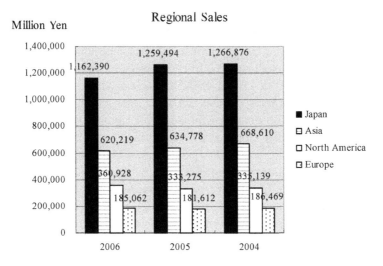

Fig. 6   Changes in regional sales
Source: SANYO (2006a).

2   Strategy and Organizational Structures

2.1   *Challenge 21 and organizational restructuring*

SANYO formulated medium-term management plans with a rolling method, and the plan used from fiscal years 2006 to 2008, developed in November 2005, is the most recent one. This section describes their new vision, "Think GAIA", and the "SANYO EVOLUTION PROJECT", including changes to the medium-term management plans. This section will discuss details about the strategy and organizational structure of SANYO as of 2004, based on interviews from 2004.

The medium-term management plan for 2001–2003, released on 26 March 2001, was named Challenge 21. Their medium-term management plan obviously changed during the target period, because it was worked out through a rolling method. Challenge 21 was aimed at accomplishing the following:

(1) Improving the company system;
(2) Changing from entity management to group management;
(3) Downsizing headquarters operations.

This plan was intended to improve the control function of headquarters operations under the company system and consider how to manage the consolidated subsidiaries as a group.

According to their website in January 2004, to achieve their goals, SANYO improved the "choice and concentration" of their businesses and management resources for the maximization of their revenue and corporate value. They needed to challenge the top businesses in the market.

To achieve the goals described, SANYO downsized the back-office section of their headquarters operation. SANYO relegated human resources and general affairs to subsidiaries established for these purposes. The controlling operation of their facilities was separated, becoming "facility services", and was relegated to another subsidiary. This action was intended to downsize the headquarters operation. Now, SANYO could enforce organizational restructuring to improve control function of their entire group. In addition, their mobile phone section's growth rose in grade, from division to company. SANYO did indeed enforce "choice and concentration" to enhance competitiveness.

Challenge 21 was the management plan until 2003; however, it was not able to achieve the plan as described in Table 1. In addition, the only areas of the company to achieve the plan through actual performance were the AV equipment segment, and the information and communication equipment segments.

2.2 *The business group system*

SANYO brought in the company system in April 1999, but during the accelerated changing of the global environment, SANYO needed to reform their entire organization, including each company and subsidiary. SANYO reformed their organization, creating four business groups, based on consumer attributes, in April 2003:

(1) Consumer Group: Products for general consumers.
(2) Commercial Group: Products and systems for businesses.

Table 1   Budget and actual performance of Challenge 21 (billions of yen)

	Budget	Actual
Operating income	165	95.5
Net income	73	13.4
ROE	9.3%	2.7%

(3) Component Group: Electric components for manufacturers.
(4) Service Group: SANYO Group logistics, financial, and service businesses centralization, utilizing the group's resources for the expansion of its earnings base.

In addition, SANYO established the International Group in April 2004, which controls the SANYO Sales and Marketing Co., Ltd. and its overseas regional headquarters. This group segments the global market into 14 regions and develops regional strategy.

Prior to this, SANYO considered their product strategy for each product group and managed their overseas strategy for each overseas headquarter subsidiary. The effect of establishing the International Group was that the manufacturing base, which had been segmented by product groups, was now able to be segmented by sales region, creating a matrix management structure.

In addition, each group was established as a company, to operate independently and gain core competence in each product: these companies were the Independence Entity, for both overseas and domestic products; the Strategy Headquarters; and the Sales & Marketing Headquarters. With this change, the company was oriented toward small-sized headquarters and reformed the function of the headquarters. They set up the Strategy Headquarters, which consisted of five units — including the Internal Audit Unit and the Strategy Unit, under the Chief Executive Officer (CEO) — and the Operation Division Staff, which consisted of 11 units, including the Accounting Unit, the Management Control Unit, and the Legal Compliance Unit, under the president and the vice presidents (COO: Chief Operating Officer; CMO: Chief Management Officer; and CFO: Chief Financial Officer). They set the technology R&D Headquarters and the Development Headquarters directly under the Head Office functions. The details of this organization are described in Figure 12.

SANYO redefined their entire organization with segments called business units, and their back-office sector, which was previously separated, was combined and operated as part of a business unit. There are 280 business units as of 31 March 2003.

The business units are classified by product line, but if a unit provides many types of products using large scale equipment, it is classified by function. Parts of the indirect operations, including the headquarters operation sector, are business units, too. The business unit of indirect operations is no longer the profit center. Now, its only function is to be the cost center.

Table 2   Chart of business description

Segmentation	Main Products
Consumer	Color television, PDP television, LCD television, Videotape recorder, DVD player, Video camera, Digital camera, LCD projector, Digital voice recorder, Car stereo, Compact disc, Facsimile, Cordless phone, Mobile phone, PHS phone, PHS cell station, Car-navigation system, LCD, DVD-ROM drive, Refrigerator, Freezer, Clothes washing machine, Cloth dryer, Microwave oven, Air conditioner, Vacuum cleaner, Electric fan, Elector massager, Dishwasher, Electrical cooking device, Toaster, Electrical rice cooker, Built-in kitchen, Electrical heater, Air purification system, Dehumidification-machine, Hybrid vehicle, Bicycle electrical component, Pump, Medical sterilizer, Medical cool box, Ultradeep freezer, Tablet packing machine, Shaver and other electrical application products
Commercial	Freezed refrigerated chilled showcase, Super-markets' showcase, Professional-use refrigerator-freezer, Ice machine, Prefabrication refrigerator-freezer, Package-type air conditioner, Gas, absorption cooling and heating machine, Medical computer, Dish cart, Electric caddie cart
Component	MOS-LSI,BIP-LSI, Thick-film IC, Liquid crystal panel, Transistor, Diode, CCD,LED, Laser diode, Optical pickup, Condenser of organic semiconductor, Other electric components, Lithium-ion battery, Nicad battery, Nickel-metal-hydride batteries, Lithium battery
Others	Credit, Logistics, Maintenance, Information Services, housing-related

Source: SANYO (2007a).

In the company's long-term vision, SANYO believes that the company and business units will be the profit center.

As described in Table 2, because each company provides multiple products, the company system that SANYO adopted before could not realize accurate profitability, because the negative earnings products and the positive earnings products were counterbalanced. However, the business unit system is a breakthrough that will remedy the difficult communication of the division's detailed information, especially bad information that existed when the company system and business division system were implemented (Hoshino, 2005, p. 65).

The business units were further segmented in April 2004, going from 271 units to 451 units. The reason for this was to clearly define the purpose of adopting the business unit system, encouraging growth, and development for the entire group through the increase and independence of the business units. In addition, it defined the evaluation process and the nature of each business unit. In 2003, each business unit was classified as one of two types, but each business has huge differences, so there will soon be five different categories (Hoshino, 2005, p. 67).

There is not a clear policy for how SANYO will increase in number of the business units. However, considering the initial purpose of segmenting the organization and the strategic goal of improving resource choices and concentrations, it seems likely that the number of the business units will fluctuate in accordance with various market situations (Figures 7–9).

Figures 10 and 11 illustrate this concept. The company can be segmented into a business unit system and a business group system, but it cannot be denied that the name of the company was only replaced to the business group. In addition, there are practical difficulties within the business unit system. For example, a president of the company or a leader of a business unit said that "everyone does the partial optimization" or "enters

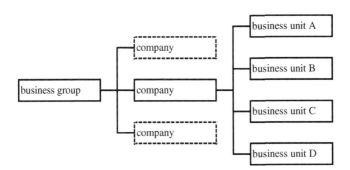

Fig. 7   Concept of the business unit
Source: SANYO (2004).

Fiscal year	Number of the business unit	Number of the company
2003	271	25
2004	451	29

Fig. 8   Changes in number of the business unit

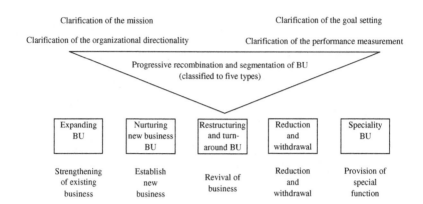

Fig. 9   Purpose for segmentation of the business unit
Source: Hoshino (2005, p. 65).

into the fox hole", and alleged that as a result, it became more difficult to operate the company than before, and team work became difficult because many people were liable to target the profits at hand (Hoshino, 2005, p. 68).

2.3   *The third business and structural change of the organization*

After SANYO suffered extensive damage by the Niigata Chuetsu Earthquake of October 2004, and because of tough competition in the field of digital appliances, SANYO's profitability decreased.

In the medium-term management plan released in November 2005, all business portfolios were reviewed, and while the previous business group and business unit systems were still used, all businesses were classified as either a core business or a business requiring structural reforms.

To conform to the slogan "Think GAIA" in this management plan, SANYO divided all businesses into the above two divisions (illustrated in Figure 12) regardless of whether the business value was high in terms of growth potential, profitability, strategic position, globalization, or core competence.

We can speculate that SANYO could reform business portfolios successfully because the previous business unit systems allowed SANYO to acquire precise information and judge investment efficiency adequately.

In addition, to realize the medium-term management plan, SANYO reformed the previous five business groups, including the International business group, into the new groups given in Table 3.

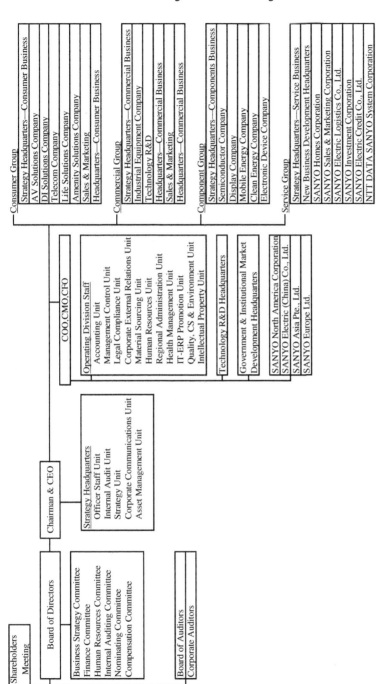

Fig. 10   Organization chart of SANYO (as of 1 April 2003)

Source: SANYO (2004).

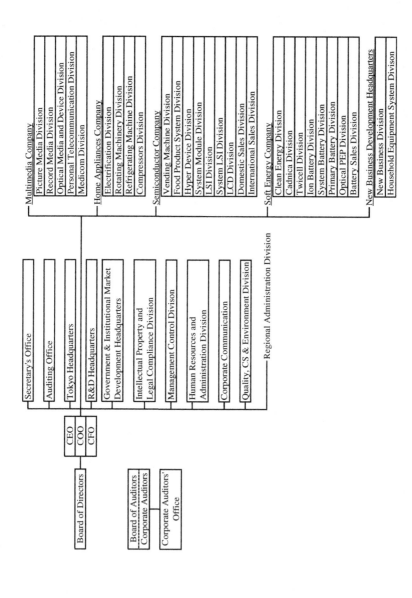

Fig. 11　Organization chart of SANYO (before 1 April 2003)

Source: SANYO (2004).

Table 3　Core business and business requiring structural reforms

	Core Business		Business Requiring Structural Reforms
Power solutions business	Secondary battery business, car electronics business, etc.	Semiconductor business	Businesses would not compete with competitors, and concentrate to develop semiconductor for AV and Power, but seek to change into profitable businesses
HVAC products & commercial equipment business	HVAC (heating, ventilating and air conditioning), Industrial Cold energy products for industrial use, photovoltaic power generation systems, compressors, biomedical equipment, medical information systems, etc.	AV equipment business centering on TV business	Businesses will archive profit increase through identification of unprofitable models, domestic sales reforms and cost structure reforms
Personal mobile device business	Mobile phone, digital camera, electronic component	Home appliance business	Businesses drastically reorganize the sales and production systems, both at home and abroad, decrease the number of product models and take measures to improve cost competitiveness
		Financial service business	Businesses aim to strengthen its financial standing and promote the autonomy of its financial services business as an independent division by establishing alliances with major partners

Source: SANYO (2007a).

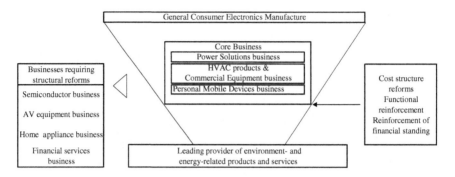

Fig. 12   Overview of medium-term management plan
Source: SANYO (2006a).

Then the financial services of the businesses requiring structural reforms were excluded from the consolidated financial statement of March 2007, after selling all company owned shares of SANYO Electric Credit Co., Ltd. to another company (Table 4). Therefore, those financial services have been excluded from organizational chart (see Figure 13) on 1 May 2007.

In addition, the semiconductor business was spun off into a separate company called SANYO Semiconductor Co., Ltd. in July 2007 in order to turn it into a self-sustaining, independent business entity capable of quickly responding to changes in the environment and to flexibly raise funds in the capital markets.

Furthermore, SANYO established a joint venture company having TV-related business functions, including planning, development, and material purchasing, with Quanta Computer Inc. in Taiwan (SANYO, 2006b).

We can speculate that the previous business group and business unit systems enabled SANYO to reform its business groups and to respond to environmental changes in rapid succession. SANYO's structural reform further clarified its strategy of selecting and focusing the company's resources.

In addition, the financial objectives of its current medium-term management plan are indicated in Table 5.

3   International Strategy and International Management Accounting

3.1   *Current condition of SANYO's international strategy*

As previously discussed, SANYO has proactively embraced the strategy of producing and selling its products overseas since the late 1940s. Moreover,

Table 4 Reforms of business group

Group before reorganization	Group after reorganization	Businesses	Division
Consumer business group	Personal mobile group	Personal mobile businesses	Core business
	Harmonious society group	Home appliance businesses	Business requiring structural reforms
		AV equipment business centering on TV business	
Commercial business group	Commercial group	HVAC products & commercial equipment businesses	Core business
	Component & device group	Semiconductor businesses	Business requiring structural reforms
Component business group	Power solution group	Power solution businesses	Core business
Service business group	Service chain group	—	—
	(SANYO Electronics Credit Co., Ltd.)	Financial business	Business requiring structural reforms
International business group	Global sales group	—	—

Source: SANYO (2007a).

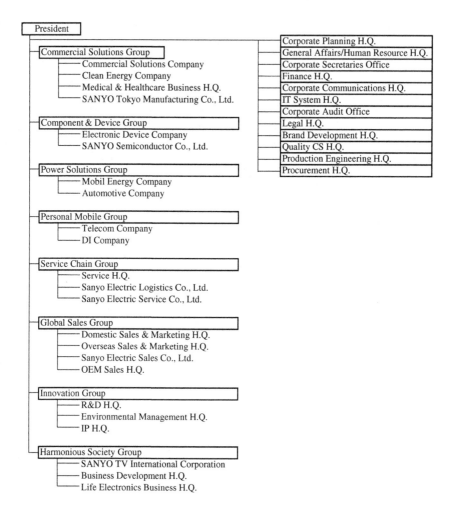

Fig. 13   Organization chart of SANYO (as of December 2006)
Source: SANYO (2007b).

in recent years it has sought to become profitable by addressing overseas strategy. For example, it has gone into partnerships and established joint ventures with successful foreign companies.

International business group, established in 2004, established 14 local areas and plotted a local strategy for each.

Thus, SANYO made full use of its global network to optimize the business model of each local market, as described below, and promoted its overseas strategy to maximize the synergistic effect of the international group.

Table 5 Medium-term management plan targets announced on 18 November 2005 (100 million yen)

	2006	2007	2008
Net sales	24,400	24,900	26,400
Operating (loss) income	(170)	750	970
(Loss) income before income taxes	(2020)	470	750
Net (loss) income	(2330)	295	620

Source: SANYO (2006a).

The main base of each local strategic area is listed below (Miyamoto and Kosuga, 2005, p. 257):

(1) *China*: In this area, which the whole world is expecting to be a good production base and market, SANYO makes use of past experience in the Chinese market to improve the business model (for example, partnership with Haier group).

(2) *Asia*: In this area, which is becoming a huge market centering on ASEAN, SANYO tries to stimulate hidden demand to provide a community-based product and service.

(3) *North America*: In this area, which is a leading global market, SANYO makes use of confidential partnerships to strengthen its presence (for example, partnership with Ford, joint ventures with Kodak, and business with Wal-Mart).

(4) *Europe*: This area has become a huge market since the accession of Eastern Europe to the European Union. Here, SANYO has competitive advantage of environmental and telecommunications technology and has developed a market for its products.

(5) *East Asia*: In this area, where the market is expected to grow up around oil-producing countries, SANYO expands its market to provide unique community-based products and services.

In 2005, in order to become a truly global company, SANYO launched the SANYO Evolution Project, based on the vision "Think GAIA." This project aimed to strengthen its sales force in foreign markets to take the No. 1 position in the areas of its core business.

Meanwhile, for businesses requiring structural reforms, SANYO tried to transfer its manufacturing operation to Asia by reducing its sales administrative expenses, cooperating with foreign countries, establishing joint-venture companies, and selling subsidiaries.

According to the current press reports, the revised medium-term management plan released in November 2006 contains plans to shift the manufacture of cell phones to Malaysia and digital cameras to Vietnam. The manufacture of refrigerators is to be turned over to Haier.

In addition, 80 manufacturing subsidiaries are to be reduced. Thus, to improve performance company-wide, an organizational restructuring currently seems to be in progress.

However, SANYO promotes not only downsizing but also co-development by linking up with foreign companies to produce high-value-added manufacturers. For example, it plans to co-develop a new refrigerator with Haier and the next generation nickel-metal-hydride battery systems for hybrid electrical vehicles with Volkswagen.

In the following section, the transition to overseas operating departments over the next several years will be described.

3.2 *Overseas operating department*

The overseas operating department was changed several times in the recent organizational restructuring. First, International business group was established in April 2004. According to the financial report released 2005, SANYO established this group because it thought that enhancement and expansion of business in foreign markets, including not only in North America, Europe, China and ASEAN, but also the Middle and Near East and Middle Asia, was required.

International business group contained regional headquarters, overseas marketing subsidiaries, overseas manufacturing subsidiaries, and overseas R&D subsidiaries. Among these, SANYO Sales & Marketing Corporation is a trading division and controls not only sales and marketing in overseas markets but also imports products manufactured in overseas factories to Japan and acts as an intermediary of import and export between overseas subsidiaries. The regional headquarters is a local office of the corporate headquarters. Whenever a local company faces a shortage of funds to invest in overseas businesses, regional headquarters provides financial support to it.

Overseas finance subsidiaries in London and New York belong to the corporate finance department. This department takes charge of company-wide tax issues and currency hedging. Corporate headquarters entrusts each company to negotiate royalties and dividends with other companies.

Before International business group was established, because each business group concentrated on manufacturing, the development of new sales markets was not seriously considered. Once International business group

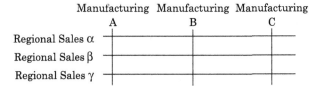

Fig. 14   Basic concept of matrix organization

was established, headquarters was able to manage the manufacturing base from the viewpoint of the regional sales base. As a result, the matrix organization illustrated in Figure 14 was structured.

The previous business group and business unit systems were reformed. Finally, the business group was reformed to eight groups and the structure of corporate headquarters was reorganized. As part of the reform, International business group was dismantled and the HA international headquarters was established to increase overseas sales.

Furthermore, under the SANYO EVOLUTION PROJECT, SANYO established a global headquarter to become a truly global company.

The Domestic sales group, overseas sales group, and OEM sales group were reorganized into the Global sales group with organizational restructuring on 1 November 2006. This group integrates domestic and international sales and marketing.

As described above, the overseas operating departments were changed many times year after year because of organizational restructuring. In 2004, SANYO established International business group, which specializes in overseas operations, to reinforce overseas business. However, this group was dismantled after only two years. We can assume that this did not reflect an abandonment of overseas business but rather was aimed at reinforcing it. In 2006, because all business groups now aimed to deploy their business globally, it was apparent that a group that specializes only in overseas operations was no longer required.

3.3 *Budgeting*

3.3.1 *Budget object organization*

SANYO identified accounting unit as a minimum object unit of budget in 2003 and collected information about revenue, expenditures, and budget from each unit. The business group and the companies who belong to the business group were an aggregate of accounting units. Before the business group system was introduced, the division or department was the accounting unit. However, when we interviewed in 2004, SANYO had been changing the accounting unit from a department to a business unit. Budget and actual information about both the company budget and the consolidated budget were collected monthly. To manage the budget and actual information, SANYO controlled all items on the income statement, but emphasized only inventory information and the depreciation cost of balance sheet items.

3.3.2 *Budgetary control*

To exercise budgetary control, basic policy about sales amounts and operating income is communicated annually in January to each company from the top management. Each company formulates the first bottom-up budget in January, the second in February and the company budget is finally based on the basic policy. Simultaneously, a capital investment plan is formulated.

After each company budget is formulated, the budgets are adjusted between companies. The business group then integrates the company budgets into the group budget and corporate headquarters formulates the master budget from a company-wide perspective.

SANYO has adopted rolling budgeting, under which a budget for three years is formulated annually. Although SANYO thinks this budgeting method is useful for determining management issues, an annual comparison of budgeted with actual has not been realized because it is difficult to predict the budget after the second year.

3.4 *SANYO Version EVA*

SANYO introduced SANYO Version EVA (SVA), a performance measurement. However, it was introduced not at the level of business units but at the level of company, because capital costs are presently too low in Japan and the difference in EVA between business units is too small to compare accurately. Since SANYO calculates not predicted but actual EVA, EVA is not used in the budget.

3.5 *Internal capital system*

SANYO introduced business-segment management system in 1986 and has been advocating each segment's independent management while emphasizing the importance of a company-wide viewpoint. The purpose of this system is to improve the management acumen of business-segment chiefs. To realize this aim, the Internal Capital System was introduced in 1986. In introducing this system, top management defined that SANYO group as an aggregation of leading medium-sized enterprises with a powerful synergistic effect (Hoshino, 2005, p. 64).

The purposes of introducing the Internal Capital System are listed below:

(1) *Succession of administrative actions as an independent corporate entity*: carrying forward profits.
(2) *Delegation of authority and clarification of responsibility*: delegate authority from corporate headquarters to the CEO of business group to a large extent.
(3) *Agile determination adapted to current condition of each business group*: determined according to financial self-analysis, investment, and business expansion.
(4) *Clarification and fair evaluation of business performance*: compared with other companies.
(5) *Identification of funds and cost of funds*: analyze use of funds and manage funds.

The basic principles of this system are as follows:

(1) *Reports of account balance*: external accounts are reported collectively in transaction department, and in-house accounts are reported in relevant departments.
(2) *Taxes and dividends*: each business segment has to bear taxes and dividends as an independent enterprise. For example, the tax assessed is 40% of the profit. In case of deficit, the tax is not assessed. On the other hand, segments need not incur costs in dividends because corporate headquarters regards dividends as a part of capital costs.
(3) *Internal interest*: head office charges 3% interest on internal transactions. However, each segment incurs 5% interest for inventory exceeding standard level, and 1% interest is charged on the value of equipment of each segment and investment amount.
(4) *Revision of standards*: standard of internal capital is revised every three years. However, the regular number of days to collect accounts receivable or to repay accounts payable is revised annually.

Internal interest is set by the Financial Headquarters and used as the capital cost of EVA across the board. Cash flows are calculated based on internal interest. To companies who embrace businesses emphasized by corporate headquarters, only 1% internal interest is charged. Each company has to create a balance sheet, income statement, cash-flow statement, and EVA for performance evaluation.

3.6 Performance evaluation of business units and companies

Each company has to create its balance sheet, income statement, cash-flow statement, and EVA. In addition, each company is evaluated according to major performance indicators to improve its profit management with an internal capital system. In the evaluation system, each performance indicator is weighted and sum of these weighted indicators is 100. Marks are calculated by the above formula (see Figure 15).

Business units are evaluated with different performance evaluations because the properties of the business units are different (see Figure 16).

(1) Specialty business units (25% of all units).
(2) Expanding business units (50% of all units).
(3) Nurturing new business units (5% of all units).
(4) Restructuring and turnaround business units (20% of all units).
(5) Reduction and withdrawal business units (transition from 4).

Numbers 2 to 5 are assumed as profit centers. Top management focuses performance evaluation indicators, such as market share, sales amount, and goal attainment level, on 2. Regarding 3, consistency with the business plan, sales growth, operating income growth, and goal attainment level are emphasized. In 4, time length for reconstruction and improvement of operating income are emphasized. With regard to 5, time length for withdrawal and balancing of deficit are emphasized. If withdrawal plans such as personnel cutbacks or sales of equipment are accelerated, the business unit is valued highly. Especially for personnel cutbacks, the amount of allowance for retirement below assumption is identified with profit contribution and the business unit are highly valued (Hoshino, 2005, p. 67). In addition, performance evaluation of business unit is implemented annually.

3.7 Management and performance evaluation of overseas business

We will discuss the performance evaluation of overseas business based on interviews with SANYO's staff members in 2004. In the case of

Marks weighted mark × $\dfrac{\text{Actual Value (A) or Standard Value (S)}}{\text{Standard Value (S) or Actual Value (A)}}$

	Key Analytical Indicator	Calculating Formula	Standard Value	Weight	Calc.	Up or Down
Profitability	Rate of return on assets	Net income ÷ total average capital × 100	4%	10	A/S	U
	Rate of return on sales	Net income ÷ amount of sales × 100	2.50%	10	A/S	U
	Achievement rate of sales	Sales amount ÷ beginning forecast of sales × 100	100%	5	A/S	U
	Achievement rate of profit	Net income ÷ beginning forecast of net income × 100	100%	5	A/S	U
	Total			30		
Efficiency	Total assets turnover	Sales amount ÷ total average capital	1.6 turns	5	A/S	U
	Tangible fixed asset turnover	Sales amount ÷ total average tangible fixed assets	5.0 turns	5	A/S	U
	Receivables turnover period	Average account receivable ÷ sales amount × 365	50 days	5	S/A	D
	Inventory turnover period	Average inventory assets ÷ sales amount × 365	20 days	5	S/A	D
	Total			20		
Productivity	Value-added per person	Value-added ÷ average number of employees	10 million yen	5	A/S	U
	Net sales per employee	Sales amount ÷ average number of employees	50 million yen	5	A/S	U
	Labor equipment ratio	Average operated tangible fixed assets ÷ average number of employees	10 million yen	5	A/S	U
	Break even ratio	Break even sales ÷ sales amount × 100	75%	5	S/A	D
	Rate of variable cost on sales	Variable cost ÷ sales amount × 100	75%	5	S/A	D
	Total			25		
Safety	Current ratio	Current assets ÷ current debt × 100	150%	5	A/S	U
	Fixed ratio	Fixed assets ÷ capital	80%	5	S/A	D
	Capital-to-asset ratio	Shareholder's equity ÷ total capital × 100	50%	5	A/S	U
	Total			15		
Growth	Growth rate for sales	(Sales amount ÷ sales amount in same period last year -1) × 100	10%	5	A/S	U
	Growth rate for profit	(Net profit ÷ net profit in same period last year -1) × 100	10%	5	A/S	U
	Total			10		
	Sum total			100		

Fig. 15   Key performance indicators

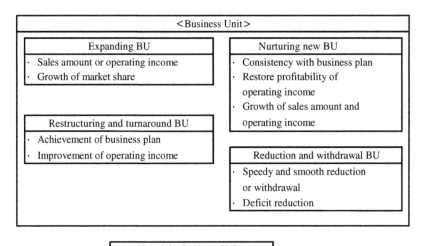

Fig. 16   Performance indicator of business unit leader
Source: Hoshino (2005, p. 66).

regional headquarters, overseas sales subsidiaries, overseas manufacturing subsidiaries, and overseas research and development subsidiaries that belong to International business group, performance was evaluated after consolidation with appropriate companies. Figure 17 shows the integration of the actual costs of overseas sales subsidiaries and income and the expenditure of the company.

However, performance of regional headquarters as overseas controlling subsidiary that established in each overseas operation was evaluated separately. Moreover, performances of overseas finance subsidiaries were evaluated not separately but along with the finance department of corporate headquarters.

Overseas businesses are planned in local currency. Therefore, comparison of planned value with actual is in local currency as well. However, corporate headquarters considers not only comparative information in local currency but also in Yens to manage across the board.

In addition, an effect of monetary inflation is not considered in evaluating performance. The corporate headquarters thinks that key point of performance evaluation is goal attainment, and the performance can be

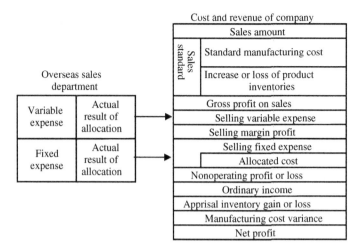

Fig. 17   Absorption of overseas sales department's expenditure into company's cost and revenue

evaluated appropriately without considering monetary inflation using unit sales or market share as performance indicators. In addition, the finance department of corporate headquarters implements anti-inflation policies such as currency hedging.

3.8 *International business alliance*

SANYO aligns not only with foreign companies of different industries such as Volkswagen, but also proactively with foreign competitors such as Samsung and Haier. The reason that SANYO seeks to align with rival companies may be, according to the interviews, that it brings the following benefits. SANYO can either:

(1) *Sell its own products though channels of partners*
    If SANYO can sell its own products through partner channels in Asian markets — including China where we can expect future exploding demand — it can achieve an effective increase of market share.
(2) *Sell its core components to partners*
    For example, SANYO can sell its core components to Haier, which has a past record of manufacturing and sales of home appliances.
(3) *Sell partners' attractive products in Japan either on an OEM basis or under the partners' brand name*

SANYO has a past record of OEM sales of digital cameras to Olympus and Nikon. Conversely, SANYO can also sell partners' products under the SANYO brand name.

(4) *Co-develop products*

For example, SANYO co-developed a global model air conditioner with Samsung Electronics. SANYO thinks that it is important to release worthwhile products quickly to survive in the highly competitive environment and it is essential for firms that collaborate to utilize one another's development resources.

(5) *Absorb methods of management*

In recent years, SANYO has absorbed methods of business unit systems from Haier, and methods of evaluating performance and the development of human resources from Samsung, and adapted them to a Japanese style to bring about an improvement of operations.

As described above, SANYO aligned with foreign competitors proactively because the alignment evaluates merits of not only the early development or reinforcement of sales channels and a reduction of manufacturing costs, but also the early development of products suitable for a global market and the absorption of excellent management methods.

4   Conclusion and Summary

This paper described the globally deployed strategy and current status of the organizational structure and the actual condition of international management accounting of SANYO Electric Co., Ltd. based on interviews. Presently, SANYO is subject to acute foreign competition and is addressing the issue of corporate rejuvenation by reforming its business structure and restructuring the organization.

To maximize enterprise value with utilization of management resources SANYO introduced a group system that aimed to move into consolidated group management. Moreover, SANYO embarked on non-manufacturing businesses including finance business to increase enterprise value. In addition, SANYO established many business units in companies to improve employee independence and hold them accountable for profit, which is vital for survival. The performance objectivity expected from each business unit was clarified by grouping business units according to strategic targets. The policy of top management to make employees independent and accountable for profit is reflected in the method of budgeting and the Internal Capital System.

Unfortunately, many of SANYO's efforts in recent years do not seem to have achieved solid results. They may require some time to succeed. However, "Eneloop", which is a representative product of the new "Think GAIA" vision, is in great demand in foreign as well as domestic markets and is expected to become a foothold for rejuvenation.

Global business restructuring, such as the reduction of manufacturing subsidiaries, is expected to continue, but the foundational rule of business restructuring are the policies "functional specialty" and "total power of group", which are determined by introducing the business group and business unit system. These two policies are supposed to be followed in the future.

A further issue for research is SANYO Version EVA. Based on our 2004 interview, because of low interest rates, EVA was not a good performance evaluation indicator of business units or companies. However, if SANYO embarks on a global marketing strategy, it is not rational to consider only domestic interest rates, and domestic rates are certainly going to increase. We will research how EVA is utilized by conducting interviews in the future.

References

Hoshino, K. (2005). Enhancement of self-reliant management of operating department, *Business Research* 970, pp. 62–68 (in Japanese).

Miyamoto, K. and Kosuga, M. (2005). Design of international management organization and management accounting, in *Design of Organization to Improve an Enterprise Value and Management Accounting*, edited by Monden, Y., Zeimukeiri-Kyokai (in Japanese).

SANYO Electric Co., Ltd. (2004). About reform of management structure and system (http://www.SANYO.co.jp/koho/hypertext4/0303news-j/0317-1.html), 26 January (in Japanese).

SANYO Electric Co., Ltd. (2006a). Annual Report 2006, SANYO Electric Co., Ltd.

SANYO Electric Co., Ltd. (2006b). About progress of SANYO Evolution Project (http://www.SANYO.co.jp/koho/hypertext4/0611news-j/1124-2.html), 24 November (in Japanese).

SANYO Electric Co., Ltd. (2007a). Annual Security Report 2006, SANYO Electric Co., Ltd. (in Japanese).

SANYO Electric Co., Ltd. (2007b). Corporate profile (http://www.SANYO.com/corporate/index.html), 23 August.

International Management Accounting in Multinational Enterprises: State-of-the-Art of Research and Practice in Japan

Masanobu Kosuga
Professor, School of Business Administration
Kwansei Gakuin University

1 Introduction

The increasing globalization of business activities in Japanese corporations during last three decades has focused attention on the several problems of accounting research and practices in Japan. Especially, financial accounting and reporting in Japanese multinational enterprises have received wide attentions by practitioners. Of course, many Japanese accounting researchers have also widely discussed international issues of financial accounting and reporting. This is clearly recognized by the growing body of accounting literatures dealing with these issues in Japan (for the details of the Japanese research trends in those days, see Hiramatsu, 1981).

Meanwhile, management accounting issues in multinational enterprises has received considerably less public attentions in the academic and/or practical literatures than have international financial accounting problems. Indeed, based on the research surveys, it is clear that research on management aspects of international accounting was lagging behind both among researchers and practitioners (Kosuga, 1983, 1988, 1993). However, the less of research in this area could be easily explained. First, management accounting is not in the public domain. Information on management accounting practices in Japanese companies is not readily available to researchers in general. Second, there are no formal standard setting bodies in management accounting areas. The development and usage of adequate management accounting systems and procedures entirely depends on the individual companies.

Needless to say, now, international and/or global management accounting is in a stage of rapid development in Japan. As the lack of international and/or global perspectives has been serious in the site of academics, the research on management accounting for multinational corporations should be made much more actively in order to realize "Relevance Regained" for management accounting research and practice in Japan.

This paper aims to contribute to the development of the subject by providing a brief summary of the survey research on international management accounting practices in Japanese multinational enterprises conducted by the Committee on International Management Accounting, Japanese Association of Management Accounting (JAMA) (Chairman: Professor Kanji Miyamoto, Osaka Gakuin University), so-called *Miyamoto Committee*. We will describe the results of the survey to provide some insights into the reality of international management accounting practices in typical Japanese corporations. To this end, several data will be provided. The next section presents the brief summary of major research issues in international and/or global dimensions of management accounting. And then, sections dealing with the major preceding researches on international and/or global dimensions of management accounting in Japan and the survey results of the JAMA Committee follow in turn. After summarizing these results, "Beyond International Management Accounting", that is to say "Towards Global Management Accounting" will be discussed.

2   The Major Research Issues in International Management Accounting

2.1   *Management control of global operations*

A multinational enterprise is a firm that has a worldwide view of R&D, production, sales, sourcing of raw materials and components, and financial markets. Different organizational structures and management philosophies toward decision-making in multinational enterprises have a great deal of influences on the management accounting system that the corporation establishes and operates. Strategies, organizational structures, and management control for global operations are most important areas in management accounting research and practices.

For example, a multinational enterprise can become multi-domestic, or it can adopt a *global strategy*. A *multi-domestic strategy* and a *global strategy* are two different strategies that companies can pursue in the global business environment. Under the *multi-domestic strategy*, each subsidiary abroad operates relatively independently of the firm as a whole, but on the other hand, under the *global strategy*, the multinational enterprise pits itself against competitors on a global, rather than market-by-market basis. The *multi-domestic strategy* allows each subsidiary abroad to operate relatively independently on a domestic-by-domestic market basis.

The major difference between these two strategies is the degree of independence held by their organizational units in implementing their strategies. The *global strategy* considers more than just the home country, and attempts to integrate global activities in order to benefit the company as a whole rather than allows each organizational unit abroad to pursue an independent strategy.

A global business strategy implies that a global accounting strategy must be developed to provide useful information to management so that they can make good decisions. Management control systems of the multinational enterprises must reflect different situations in each of the countries where it operates. The systems must be appropriate for the sophistication of the individual countries, and they must also satisfy the needs of the firm as a whole.

2.2 *Organizational structures: Centralization vs. decentralization*

Every multinational enterprise is confronted with opportunities and obstacles in its quest for creating corporate value. One way of benefiting from opportunities and finding off obstacles is to achieve the appropriate fit between corporate strategies, organizational design, and management control systems. The problem with centralization vs. decentralization is the most important element for the multinational enterprises to carry out their own global strategies. In the case of Matsushita Electric Industrial Co., Ltd., centralized organization and decentralized organization have been swinging from side to side like a pendulum in a clock (for the details of Matsushita's case, see Pascale and Athos, 1982; Abegglen and Stalk, 1985; Monden, 1985; Fushimi, 1989; Kono and Clegg, 2001; Miyamoto *et al.*, 2005; Miyamoto and Kosuga, 2006; Kosuga, 2007).

According to Bartlett and Ghoshal (1989), three global imperatives are identified. They influence organizational structure, the degree of centralization/decentralization of managerial decision-making, and the organizational culture of the firm. These imperatives are as follows:

(a) *Forces for global integration*: the need for efficiency. Companies need to achieve economies of scale and scope in areas such as product lines, parts design, and manufacturing operations. These economies are driven for cost reasons as well as by more harmonized tastes and preferences of customers.

(b) *Force for local differentiation*: the need for responsiveness. Different market structures, customers' preference and/or wants, and government interference require closer attention to local differences.

(c) *Forces for worldwide innovation*: the need for learning. This imperative involves developing and diffusing worldwide innovations, and linking and leveraging knowledge.

Every multinational enterprise needs to deal with all three imperatives rather than focus on just one. In the previous section, we discussed companies as being *multi-domestic type* or *global type*. *Multi-domestic type* is focusing more on country differences, and *global type* is focusing more on strategies crossing national borders. Bartlett and Ghoshal (1989) stated that firms needed to move to what they call a *transnational approach* in order to deal most effectively with these three imperatives. In this approach stated by Bartlett and Ghoshal, corporate assets are dispersed, interdependent, and specialized. This is quite different from both *multi-domestic type* companies and *global type* companies. *Multi-domestic type* companies are decentralized and independent, and *global type* companies are highly centralized globally scaled.

Based on the transnational organizational philosophy advocated by Bartlett and Ghoshal, the accounting function also would be affected strongly. Managers in multinational enterprises need to legitimize, diverse perspectives and capabilities, and develop multiple and flexible coordination process in order to become globally competitive and flexible in the multinational competitive markets (for the details, see Bartlett and Ghoshal, 1989, pp. 65–67).

From this point of view, it would appear that the multinational enterprise would need to have a management information system that provides a significant amount of information, which flows from the head office to foreign subsidiaries, from subsidiaries to the parent, and among the subsidiaries and/or affiliates. That is quite different from highly decentralized operations and highly centralized operations.

2.3 *Strategic management information systems*

Information system for strategic management also has to be suited to the organizational structure and management philosophy of the multinational enterprise. A company that operates through a highly decentralized structure under a *multi-domestic strategy* has quite different requirements for management information and control from those of a highly centralized firm that operates under a *global strategy*. Considerably autonomous subsidiaries and affiliates do not require as much control from the head office of the parent firm. Therefore, they need not present frequent feedback information to the parent.

Needless to say, the transition from multinational or multi-domestic to global involves a change or development in the mix of mechanisms required for the companies in order to coordinate their efforts. In general, historical evolution in the use of mechanisms of coordination among multinational enterprises is classified into three stages. They are as follows:

(a) Stage 1: "Multinational" and "Multi-domestic"
(b) Stage 2: "Global" and "Pure Global"
(c) Stage 3: "Transnational" and "Complex Global"

Structural configuration or organizational patterns of multinational enterprises in Stage 1 is *Decentralized Federation*. Its characteristic is loose federation of highly autonomous national subsidiaries, each focused primarily on its local market. Main formal mechanisms and organizational structures for coordination utilized by multinational enterprises in Stage 1 are (1) international division; (2) direct personal reporting; (3) not much output control (i.e., results control) and mainly financial performance; and (4) behavioral control (i.e., action control) by using expatriate executives.

Structural configuration or organizational patterns of multinational enterprises in Stage 2 is *Centralized Hub*. Its characteristic is centralized value activities that provide the company a competitive advantage (normally upstream activities, such as product design or manufacturing). These activities are centralized at headquarters of the parent firm, or are tightly controlled. Main formal mechanisms and organizational structures for coordination utilized by multinational enterprises in Stage 2 are (1) international division, worldwide product, geographic, or regional division; (2) higher centralization of decision-making at headquarters of the parent company; (3) higher formalization of policies, rules, and procedures; (4) standardization in planning and budgeting systems; and (5) tight output control in the United States multinational enterprises, and behavioral (and cultural) control in Japanese multinational enterprises.

Structural configuration or organizational patterns of multinational enterprises in Stage 3 is *Integrated Network*. In this type, physical assets and management capabilities are distributed internationally to country units, thus creating a truly integrated network of dispersed yet interdependent resources and capabilities. Each subsidiary is considered a source of ideas, skills, and knowledge. Main formal mechanisms and organizational structures for coordination utilized by multinational enterprises in Stage 3 are (1) formal structures plus global matrix; (2) centralization of decision-making but upgrading the role of subsidiaries; (3) high formalization; (4) strategic planning; and (5) tight and complex output control. And more informal and subtle mechanisms in Stage 3 are (1) temporary or permanent teams, task forces, committees, integrators; (2) informal channels of communication and relationships among all managers; and (3) strong organizational culture by knowing and sharing objectives and values.

In short, how to coordinate the increasing number of dispersed and yet interdependent international activities in multinational enterprises are most important matter for managers. In general, we have two ways in order to coordinate the activities of multinational enterprises; one is through structural and formal mechanism, and the other is through more informal and subtle mechanism. The relevance, adequacy, suitability, and timeliness of the information system for implementing strategic management are all key determinants of the success of decision-making and control systems in multinational enterprises. A solid strategic management information system is needed to provide the information that is necessary to the more formal reporting structure and to provide information that makes the informal and subtle control systems work.

2.4 *Performance evaluation, and budgetary planning and control*

The fourth issue is the ways to evaluate performance of managers and organizational units in the international context. Multinational enterprises generally tend to use the same measures in order to evaluate performance of domestic and foreign operations. Major problems related to performance evaluation are as follows:

(a) *Desirability and advisability of using multiple bases for performance measurement*: different criteria and measures for different kinds of operations in different countries.

(b) *Choice of currency in which to evaluate performance*: "before-translation" basis is more likely to be used by a multinational enterprise seeking global optimization. Which currency to use (the local currency or the parent currency) is one of the issues surrounding the preparation of budgets for the multinational enterprises.

(c) *Controllability*: whether a foreign currency rises or falls in value is obviously beyond the control of a multinational enterprise.

(d) *Budgetary planning and control for global operations*: which dimensions of international environment and the firm's global strategy that might affect the budgetary planning and control process, in which currency should the budget be prepared, and how should the foreign currency factor be dealt with when translating the budget from the local currency into the parent currency.

(e) *Transfer pricing for foreign subsidiaries in highly integrated multinational enterprises*: different purposes for the existence of the foreign subsidiaries cause the transfer pricing problems.

It is quite important to determine which measures for performance evaluation should be developed in the local currency or the parent currency. Based on the logical thinking, the local currency seems to be fairer to the local manager, but the parent currency is also very important because top management of the multinational enterprises needs to answer to several kinds of shareholders based on parent currency performance.

In developing a global budgeting process, it is important to take the next two factors into consideration; they are the different dimensions of the international environment, and the global strategy implemented by the multinational enterprises. They might have an influence on the budgetary planning and control process, in which currency the budget should be prepared, and how the foreign currency factor should be dealt with when translating the budget from the local currency into the parent currency. Organizational and/or national culture, attitude toward performance evaluation, transfer pricing, rapidly changing economic environments have significant influences on the budgetary planning and control process in the multinational enterprises.

Besides these matters, there are a few issues related to carrying the global strategy into execution. They are as follows:

(a) Global production strategies implementing in the global competitive environment and multinational manufacturing systems: to what extent are there differences in approaches as between multinational enterprises based in different countries.

(b) Tax rates: different rates worldwide influence the companies to allocate expenses and assets in order to minimize the overall tax liability, subject to the constraints of the national tax authorities.
(c) International banking and financial services.
(d) International communications and information technology.

So far, several research books and articles in Japan have introduced some ideas of organizational structures and management control systems for multinational enterprises in Japan and explained how these ideas have been implemented and debated in the United States, United Kingdom, and other Western countries. However, not enough attention has been paid to the practical aspects of Japanese companies. The past studies in Japan have not answered the questions such as which type of organizational design and structures did Japanese enterprises construct in terms of the extent of decentralization?; what kind of management control systems did they establish?; and how did they use accounting information for global value-based management? In the next section, we will examine the major research books on international management accounting, which were published in Japanese, in order to make clear the state-of-the-art of the research in Japan.

3   Major Researches in Japan: 1980–2007

3.1   *Goals of research*

In general, the word "research" means a critical process for asking and attempting to answer questions about the world. According to Dane (1990), the ultimate goals of research are to formulate questions and to find answers to these questions, and the immediate goals of research are (1) exploration, (2) description, (3) prediction, (4) explanation, and (5) action. From this point of view, research is able to classified into five types. They are as follows:

(a) Type 1: Exploration (does it exist?)
(b) Type 2: Description (what is it, and how is it different?)
(c) Type 3: Prediction (what is it related to?)
(d) Type 4: Explanation (what causes it?)
(e) Type 5: Action (how can research be put to use?)

Exploratory research involves an attempt to determine whether or not a phenomenon exists. Descriptive research involves examining a phenomenon to more fully and more carefully define it or differentiate it from other phenomena. Prediction is an important goal of research. It means identifying relationships that enable us to speculate about one thing by knowing about some other thing. Explanatory research involves examining a cause–effect relationship between two or more phenomena. Therefore, it is used to determine whether or not an explanation (cause–effect relationship) is valid or to determine which of two or more competing explanation is most valid. Action research refers to a kind of researches which is conducted in order to solve a social problem (for the details of implications of the research, see Dane, 1990, pp. 3–19).

In the area of international management accounting in Japan, most of the research are Type 1 and/or 2 (for the details of Japanese management accounting research and practices in general, see Monden and Sakurai, 1989; Yoshikawa *et al.*, 1994; Sakurai and Scabrough, 1995, 1997; Monden, 2000; Okano and Suzuki, 2007). This is the feature of Japanese research at present. The following sections will indicate it.

3.2   *Pioneering researcher, Professor Miyamoto*

Professor Kanji Miyamoto (Osaka Gakuin University) is a pioneer in the international management accounting research in Japan. He published the first research book on international management accounting theory in Japan, titled *Fundamentals of International Management Accounting*, in 1983. In this book, he presented the theoretical framework for international transfer pricing models based on a wide range of foreign literature review. Different transfer prices for different purposes — this is the most important proposition in this book (Miyamoto, 1983).

In 1989, Miyamoto published the second research book, titled *Management Accounting for Multinational Enterprises*. He examined the several research results published abroad. His focus is on some factors that affect performance evaluation systems in multinational enterprises (Miyamoto, 1989). They are as follows:

(a) Organizational structure;
(b) Foreign currency and exchange rate risk;
(c) Inflation;
(d) Several environmental factors.

Miyamoto clarified the traditional research areas of international management accounting and established the theoretical framework for Japanese researchers. And, in 2003, he published his third research book, titled, *Management Accounting in Global Enterprises*. Miyamoto (2003) compiled his many years of research into this book. The feature of this book is the strategic-orientation, especially based on *Transnational Strategy* advocated by Bartlett and Ghoshal (1989).

After the publication of this book, he began to conduct the field research as a chairman of JAMA Committee (i.e., *Miyamoto Committee*) in order to clarify the present state of international management accounting practices in Japanese multinational enterprises. The results of this Committee will be discussed in the next section.

3.3   *Major researches in the 1990s*

In the mid-1990s, two noteworthy research books were published in Japan. They are the Collected-Papers type books. One is *Globalization of Business Enterprises and Management Accounting* edited by Professor Yoshihiro Itou (Waseda University, Tokyo) in 1995; the other is *Global Business and Accounting: Managerial, Financial, and Governmental* edited by Professors Hiroshi Yoshida (Emeritus Professor, Hyogo Prefectural University, Kobe) and Kenji Shiba (Kansai University, Osaka) in 1997.

The former book (Itou, 1995) consists of 13 chapters. The major issues dealt with are as follows:

(a) Basic issues in global management accounting.
(b) Actual circumstances of the globalization of Japanese enterprises, based on the questionnaire survey.
(c) Budgeting.
(d) Performance evaluation of foreign subsidiaries.
(e) Transferability of target costing mechanisms aboard.
(f) International transfer pricing.
(g) Management control in the multinational enterprises.
(h) Five Case Researches of Japanese firms.
(i) Global management accounting: past, present, and future.

The latter book (Yoshida and Shiba, 1997) consists of 16 chapters. The major issues dealt with are as follows:

(a) Influences of globalization on management and accounting.
(b) Issues in management accounting for global organizational structures: practice, education, and research.

(c) Corporate strategy and accounting in global organizational structure.
(d) Organizational structure and accounting in the network society.
(e) Target costing in the foreign subsidiaries.
(f) Performance evaluation in the global organizations.
(g) Case research of Matsushita Electric Industrial Co., Ltd.
(h) Environmental management issues in the global enterprises.
(i) Exchange rates risk and accounting.
(j) Issues of the globalization of Japanese enterprises.
(k) International financing in Japanese enterprises.
(l) International transfer pricing.
(m) Taxation problems.

The noteworthy characteristic of them is that the research focuses were concentrated on Japanese companies. In those days, many Japanese scholars started to make efforts in order to conduct not only foreign literature review, but also Japanese field surveys and case researches.

3.4 Major researches in the first decade of the 21st century

After 2000, we have now four excellent Japanese research books on management accounting for multinational enterprises. They are as follows:

(a) Hiroshi Okano (Professor, Osaka City University), *Global Strategy and Accounting*, in 2003.
(b) Kazunori Itou (Professor, Senshu University, Tokyo), *Global Management Accounting*, in 2004.
(c) Masaru Nakagawa (Professor, Doshisha University, Kyoto), *Globalization of Management Accounting*, in 2004.
(d) Susumu Ueno ed. (Professor, Konan University, Kobe), *Management Accounting Practices among Japanese MNEs: Finding from a Mail Questionnaire Survey*, in 2007.

First, Okano's work is the international comparative case studies on cost management practices (mainly target costing practices in the United States and Japan) in the product development phase (Okano, 2003). He tried actively to clarify the features of Japanese management accounting and/or Japanese style of managerial usage of accounting information.

Next, Itou's work is notable, because this book shows Japanese academician's common sense in those days, on global dimensions of management accounting research and practices (Itou, 2004). He summarized almost all the research results, based on a wide range of the preceding literature review and his own case researches on large Japanese manufacturing companies (Nissan, Toshiba, Denso, and so on).

Nakagawa's work is also noteworthy (Nakagawa, 2004). His research focus is concentrated on the management accounting systems that operate in the foreign manufacturing subsidiaries of Japanese multinational enterprises. Main research issues dealt with in his questionnaire surveys are: cost management, target costing, standard costing, management control, budgeting, and R&D management. And the United States, Europe, and Thailand were selected for the regions where research subjects (i.e., Japanese firms' subsidiaries) were operating. This questionnaire survey is the first and most rigid "hypothesis-test" type research on management accounting practices in Japanese multinational enterprises.

Ueno's edited book (Ueno, 2007) shows the research results conducted by JAMA Committee on "Management Accounting Practices in Japanese Multinational Enterprises" (Chairman: Professor Susumu Ueno). This is the "fact-finding" type research, based on a mail questionnaire survey. Management accounting practices among Japanese multinational enterprises in general, international transfer pricing, applications of IT, performance evaluation, and international capital budgeting are treated as main research issues in this survey.

In this section, we examined the major Japanese research books on management accounting research and practice in Japanese multinational enterprises published during the last two decades. From the literature review done in this section, it is very clear that Japanese academic efforts were started in order to revive the relevance and usefulness of management accounting research in Japan since the mid-1990s. These efforts seem to have two directions. One is the active implementation of much more field surveys and case researches. In the late 1980s, as to the characteristics of Japanese management accounting research, it was indicated that field studies were only a few, and empirical researches were few (for the details, see Kosuga, 1983, 1988). However, during the last decade, more field surveys, empirical researches, and case researches have taken place as to the global aspects of management accounting practices in Japanese multinational enterprises.

The other is the positive academic effort to introduce Japanese researches and/or practices to foreign researchers and practitioners. Of course, the aim of this book is also the same. It is hoped that this paper will help the non-Japanese researchers in their endeavor to understand the current research and practices in Japan. English language materials on Japanese management accounting research as well as practices are still quite limited.

4   Summary and Discussion of *Miyamoto Committee's* Results on International Management Accounting Practices in Japan

4.1   *Case 1: Matsushita Electric Industrial Co., Ltd.*

Based on the survey of several publications, the semi-structured interview method was used in the *Miyamoto Committee*'s study. Interviewees were senior financial directors, chief operating officers, and managers of planning department in the head office in Osaka, Japan. The Committee tried to clarify how Matsushita has implemented strategic management control for global operations during the last decade. The recent reconstruction of global management system implemented by Matsushita is as follows:

(1) In January 1994, *Regeneration Plan* (a middle-range business plan) and the *Business Group System* (the *Division–Group System* were started. The Business Group System was established by grouping its divisions into some product-based groups and adding separate marketing, administrative, and R&D functions to them) was abolished. The *Divisional System* was revived to promote the agile decision-making, quick response, and its speedy implementation under the direct supervision of the president.

(2) In April 1997, *Progress 2000 Plan* was launched. At the same time, *Internal Division Company System* (what is called, *Company System* in Japan) was launched. Four internal *Bunsha* (intra-companies like as previous *Business Groups*) were established. By implementing these strategies, Matsushita had been trying to work in order to enhance capital efficiency through the utilization of *Capital Cost Management* (CCM), which was introduced in 1999. CCM is a Matsushita's own yardstick for internal divisional management control, and it is a kind of a residual income. The balance of operating assets multiplied by cost of capital set at 8.4% is the cost of assets invested.

(3) In April 2001, *Value Creation 21* was started. It was the next mid-term plan, which was designed to take full advantage of the opportunities created by evolving digital networking society. The goal of this plan

was to transform Matsushita into a Super Manufacturing Company, which would provide truly customer-oriented services as its principal mission through the development and supply of systems, equipment, and devices.

(4) In January 2003, Matsushita reorganized their group structure to maximize corporate value of the entire Matsushita Group as a whole. This system is called the *Business Domain System (Multi-Business Domain System)*. *Business Domain* is a large strategic business unit. The aims of this business restructuring were to provide the most effective solution services from a customers' point of view, to eliminate counterproductive overlapping of businesses among group companies, to concentrate and make optimum use of group-wide R&D resources, and to establish an integrated operational structure that covers everything from product development and manufacturing to sales, thereby ensuring a pertinent autonomous management structure (Matsushita, 2002, p. 5). Indeed, this structural reformation was designed to "deconstruct" management structures of the 20th century and "create" business and products that would lead to future growth. The key features of this new structure were empowerment (delegation of authority) and capital governance. Under this new organizational structure, all business domain companies were established as the customer-oriented, autonomous organizations.

(5) The business domain companies have complete authority over, and must take responsibility for all aspects of business activities in their respective domain, including not only domestic but also overseas operations, from R&D and manufacturing, to sales. By delegating such responsibilities, Matsushita tried to promote autonomous management by each business domain company, thus accelerating decision-making, and facilitating efficient allocation of management resources. The role of the Headquarters is to oversee these operations from a shareholder's perspective.

(6) In 2004, Matsushita implemented further reform to establish an optimum management and governance structure tailored to the Group's new business and organizational structure. Under the new structure, the Headquarters empower each of the business domain companies by delegating authority in order to expedite autonomous management (Matsushita, 2003, p. 10). The aims of this restructuring were to eliminate business duplications, to integrate R&D, manufacturing and sales, and to concentrate R&D resources.

(7) To increase the effectiveness of these reforms, Matsushita created a framework for capital governance in a new management system. The company revised the fundamental components of the previous internal divisional management system: Headquarters Fee Structure, Internal Share Investment/Dividend System, and Business Performance Evaluation Standards (Matsushita, 2003, p. 9). First, charges paid to the headquarters were treated as variable under the previous system, because they were calculated based on sales amount. This treatment has been changed. They are now fixed in accordance with services provided by the headquarters. Second, a new standard regarding internal dividends was started, in which each business domain company pays dividends to the headquarters at a fixed rate, based on the domain company's consolidated shareholder's equity. Under this system, business domain companies are required to pay dividends whether or not they are profitable, thereby providing an incentive for closure/integration of unprofitable business. Furthermore, Matsushita introduced a new overseas share investment system, where business domain companies deposit funds with the headquarters in an amount equivalent to the share investment in the relevant overseas subsidiaries under their control, and in turn, the headquarters, through regional headquarter companies, invests 100% in shares of such overseas subsidiaries. With this new system, business domain companies are effectively responsible for not only investment but also management of overseas subsidiaries in their domain (Matsushita, 2003, p. 9). Finally, Matsushita revised the performance evaluation measures for business domain companies to promote autonomous management and allow for effective delegation of authority. Their performance is evaluated based on two results-based measurements. They are CCM for evaluating capital efficiency and cash flows for evaluating a company's ability to generate cash. Both of these measures are applied to each business domain company's performance on a global consolidated basis (Matsushita, 2003, p. 9). Through these management system reforms, business domain companies are shifting from the parent-alone, domestic focus of the past, to an autonomous management style that emphasizes cash flow on a global consolidated basis (Matsushita, 2003, p. 9). Furthermore, compensation for members of the Board of Directors and Executive Officers is linked to this new performance evaluation measures to pursue management based on shareholder interests and enhance corporate value.

(8) After *Value Creation 21* plan ended on 31 March 2004, Matsushita started the next mid-term plan called *Leap Ahead 21*. The aim of this plan is to achieve global excellence by 2010 to fulfill its mission of creating value for customers. Overseas Initiative within the *Leap Ahead 21* plan is a vital role of overseas operations as a "growth engine" in expanding business and enhancing overall earnings.

(9) Mr. Yukio Shohtoku, former Executive Vice President (Member of the Board) in charge of Overseas Operations, said that key strategies for future growth were (i) a unified global brand, (ii) matrix management, (iii) superior products, (iv) realizing ¥1000 billion business in China, and (v) creation of a "lean and agile" marketing structure. Figure 1 shows the structure for matrix management (Matsushita, 2004, p. 13). Matsushita has expanded the responsibilities of regional headquarter companies to include corporate governance functions regarding overseas operations. Mr. Shohtoku said, "As a result, overseas subsidiaries are included not only in the consolidated operations of their respective business domain companies, but are also part of the regional consolidated management of regional headquarter companies. Overseas

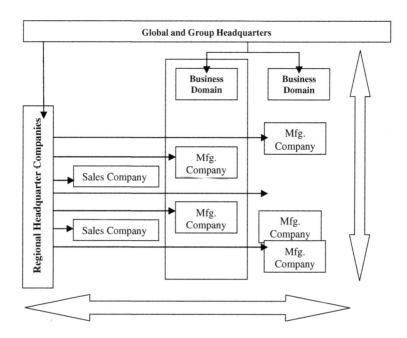

Fig. 1   Business domain companies and regional headquarter companies

operations are thus managed according to a matrix with a 'business axis' for the global strategies of business domains, and a 'region axis' for the comprehensive growth strategies of regional headquarter companies" (Matsushita, 2004, pp. 12–13). Vertical "business axis" shows the globally consolidated management by business domain companies, and horizontal "region axis" shows the regionally consolidated management by regional headquarter companies.

4.2 *Case 2: Sharp Corporation*

Based on the survey of several publications, the semi-structured interview method was used in this *Miyamoto Committee*'s study. The Committee tried to clarify how Sharp has implemented strategic management control for global operations. Main findings are as follows:

(1) Sharp has adopted the Divisional Organization System. This system consists of *Head Office Group*, *Business Group*, and others. A *Business Group* is an investment center and each *Business Group* holds some divisions. As a division is a profit center, each division produces and sells its own products and components. *Head Office Group* consists of some staff groups, planning groups, and Tokyo Branch Office.

(2) Regarding sales activities, the domestic sales subsidiaries are directed and managed by the *Domestic Sales and Marketing Group*, and the oversea sales subsidiaries are directed and controlled by the *International Business Group*. Sharp Trading Corporation was established as a subsidiary company that provides several services to all import/export activities in Sharp as a whole. All transfer transactions among overseas business units are executed through this company.

(3) Each division belongs to a *Business Group*, and each *Business Group* has its own factory. Therefore, every product of the divisions is manufactured there. The aim of this system is to make Sharp production system adaptable, agile, and responsive to the market. Sharp has adopted a *Global Product Division Structure* in which each division is responsible for its global performance. And Sharp has also adopted an International Divisional Structure, which is similar to the manufacturing system. *International Business Group* is responsible for the global performance. As there is no regional head office, sales subsidiaries overseas act as a regional support office. Overseas sales performed by subsidiaries are managed by the *Head Office* of the parent in Japan.

(4) Based on a middle-range business plan for three years, the *Head Office* formulates a short-range business plan, and then makes several budget guidelines for preparing an operating budget. Six-months type budget is prepared based on the bottom-up budgeting process. Each business unit in Sharp (i.e., *Business Groups*, divisions, sales and manufacturing subsidiaries and so on) is managed under a rolling budget, and transfer prices are negotiated and used in the budgeting process between overseas subsidiaries and domestic divisions.

(5) As all divisions are treated as a profit center, they prepare their own budgeted income statement. Each *Business Group* as an investment center prepares a set of budgeted financial statements (i.e., income statement, balance sheet, and cash flow statement).

(6) Sharp uses ROA, ROE, and free cash flow as principal financial indicators for performance evaluation. Performance of each business unit is measured in terms of sales, operating income, several kinds of expense rates, balance of inventory, balance of receivables and so on. The most important measures are sales and operating income both in planning and for performance evaluation.

(7) In 2000, an internal capital system was introduced in order to manage *Business Groups* since 2000, and "Profit after Capital Cost" was also introduced as a kind of performance measures.

(8) Foreign subsidiaries are authorized to conduct financing activities independently from the parent. Dividends from foreign subsidiaries have to be paid at a rate of 50% of their profit to *Head Office*. In addition, each foreign subsidiary is charged royalty based on sales, with specific expenses being allowed on the basis of several supporting activities from *Head Office*.

4.3   *Case 3: SANYO Electric Co., Ltd.*

Based on the survey of several publications, the semi-structured interview method was used in this *Miyamoto Committee*'s study. The Committee tried to clarify how SANYO has implemented strategic management control for global operations during the last decade. The recent reconstruction of global management system implemented by SANYO is as follows:

(1) In 1999, SANYO introduced *Business Headquarter Company System* to reinforce the function of traditional divisional organizations. Eight headquarters were reorganized into five in-house company groups.

(2) In 2003, based on the mid-term business plan called *Challenge 21*, SANYO reformed its business organizations into four customer-oriented *Business Groups*. Former Chairman & CEO, Satoshi Iue said, "With our planned conversion to a holding company structure in mind, we have reorganized our head office into a strategy *Headquarters Division* and *Operating Division* staff and further divided these divisions into business units. The strategy Headquarters Division will eventually be transferred to the holding company, and the Staff Division will be divided up among the entities of the SANYO Group, primarily the business companies. Overseas business development strategies, too, will be transferred to business groups, with the function and role of the resulting new sections to be determined by region in accordance with the trend to greater autonomy and responsibility" (SANYO, 2003, p. 6). Structural reforms resulted in better profit structures. In fact, SANYO intended to use those transformations aggressively and continually to raise its profitability, to create positive corporate value and brand value, to gain a sufficient free cash flow, and to create a strong, highly competitive structure.

(3) In order to create a powerful, self-reliant group, SANYO divided the Group into 271 *SANYO Business Units* (SBUs, or simply BUs) along product, functional lines, business process, and regions. SBUs have clearly defined goals and lines of responsibility, make it easy to judge each unit profitability (sales, profit, profit ratio) or contribution to the total profitability, and encourage a simple and quick decision-making to improve their agility.

(4) SANYO started a new management system in 2003. The system was established based on the following basic concepts:

(a) *Business Groups* are responsible for operations in their respective fields.

(b) They are obligated to contribute to maximizing the corporate value of the entire SANYO group.

(c) In-house companies are treated as profit centers, and are responsible both for business in their fields and for the management of BUs under them. BUs, in turn, are responsible for achieving the business goals determined for them by their in-house company's plan and for contributing to the business performance of the in-house company.

(5) In fiscal year 2004, SANYO expanded *Business Groups* to five. *International Business Group* was added. As a result of this structural

reform, Headquarters (comprises 54 BUs), Consumer Business Group (124 BUs), Commercial Business Group (59 BUs), International Business Group (26 BUs), Components Business Group (109 BUs), and Service Business Group (79 BUs) were established. A further clarification of roles and directions yielded 451 BUs in April 2004.

(6) The mission of *International Business Group* is "to provide the products and services of each Business Group tailored to local markets" (SANYO, 2004, p. 5). This group was established to focus on developing business overseas. SANYO intended to strengthen its international presence through integrating overseas operations.

(7) On 1 April 2005, SANYO implemented organizational reformation again to further evolve their management systems. The company was reorganized into the eight Business Groups to clarify SANYO's future priority business domains. These groups are Home Electronics Group, Personal Electronics Group, Component and Device Group, Power Solutions Group, Commercial Solutions Group, Sales and Marketing Group, Innovation Group, and Business and Management Group. The focus of this reformation is on the "Subdivision and Reorganization of the previous *Business Groups* and *Business Unit Systems* into the eight Business Groups" and the "Realization of a small, strong Headquarters." The purposes of this reformation are "to quickly cope with the rapid and severe changes in the management climate, to become a more customer- and market-oriented company, and to facilitate speedy decision-making" (SANYO, 2005, p. 6). As a result of this structural reform, *International Business Group* was deconstructed. It means that SANYO backed away from a global matrix organization and now stays at a global product division stage.

(8) In September 2005, SANYO stated that SANYO would establish the *Global Headquarter* to reform this new business group system. This reformation is recognized as getting back to the global matrix organization stage from a global division stage.

(9) SANYO introduced new control systems. SANYO started to use some performance measures to evaluate the results of *Business Groups* and in-house companies. SANYO uses profitability and growth as its evaluation criteria. They are based on income statement, balance sheet, cash flow statement, and SVA (SANYO's version of residual income like as economic value-added). SVA is calculated as follows:

$$SVA = \text{After tax income} - \text{Cost of capital.}$$

Cost of capital is usually 3% of the total of interest-bearing debt and capital. SVA is used as an *ex post* measure for in-house company level performance evaluation, neither as an *ex ante* nor for BUs. Performance measures for BUs are based on major items in income statement. BU is the smallest unit to which SANYO applies its evaluation criteria.

5 Summary of the Results

In this section, we summarized the results of the interview research. The major findings are as follows:

(1) The core of the global strategy is to maximize corporate value.
(2) The major role of headquarters is to develop and coordinate subsidiaries strongly in an integrated effort. Tax and financial issues are treated at headquarters.
(3) The major role of subsidiaries and in-house companies is to carry out and support a detailed strategy developed at the business domain company or the *Business Group.*
(4) Matsushita has a global matrix organization, Sharp has a global product division structure, and SANYO has a business group-based organizational structure like a global product division structure.
(5) But, in September 2005, SANYO stated that SANYO would establish the *Global Headquarter* to reform this new business group system.
(6) Matsushita uses quite simple performance measures: CCM and free cash flow. SANYO uses a variety of financial measures. Sharp uses several financial indicators.
(7) Local currency is basically used for planning and controlling overseas operations.

Needless to say, the study conducted by the *Miyamoto Committee* is a case-based research that involves the collection of some types of evidence: documentary evidence (historical documents and archival evidence) and semi-structured interview data. According to Yin (1984), a case study means an empirical inquiry that investigates a contemporary phenomenon within its real life context when the boundaries between the phenomenon and its context are unclear, and where multiple sources of evidence are used.

From this point of view, the aim of this Committee's research is "fact finding" only. Therefore, the weakness of this research is apparent. It is the lack of direct observation (i.e., observation of physical traces and systematic observation) and participant observation (for the details of the case study methods in management accounting research, see Brownell, 1995, pp. 59–77).

To conduct much more rigid research on international management accounting practices in Japanese multinational enterprises based on these research results, we must reconsider which type of research methods is most suitable for the research: experimental research, quasi-experimental research, survey research, field research, or archival research. In order to enhance the validity of the research, we must do such an effort as quickly as possible.

6   Conclusion: Towards *Global Management Accounting*

The research theme of *Miyamoto Committee* is "International Management Accounting." But, the name *International Management Accounting* is too old or too traditional to make much more rigid research from now on. *Global Management Accounting* is the most suitable expression at present, so-called "Beyond International Management Accounting" and "Towards Global Management Accounting." So as to realize *Relevance Regained*, global management accounting research and practices in Japan need to be updated and modified to accommodate the novel and different information-related needs of managers in Japanese multinational enterprises.

In this paper, we correlated organizational structures with their guiding global strategies and supported management control systems. The major findings are as follows:

(1) As Lawrence and Lorsch (1967) previously stated, centralization vs. decentralization is an irresolvable conflict and the excellent company must have both.
(2) Matsushita and SANYO continuously carry out organizational reform to ensure their organizational vitality.
(3) Matsushita and SANYO continuously try to adapt their organizational structures to the changing environment.
(4) Matsushita uses quite simple performance measures — CCM and free cash flows — to manage its business domain companies. Sharp and SANYO use much more detailed financial indicators for performance evaluation.

References

Abegglen, J. C. and Stalk, G. (1985). *Kaisha: The Japanese Corporation*, New York: Harper & Row.

Bartlett, C. A. and Ghoshal, S. (1989). *Managing Across Borders*, Boston, Massachusetts: Harvard Business School Press.

Brownell, P. (1995). *Research Methods in Management Accounting*, Coopers & Lybrand Accounting Research Methodology Monograph No. 2, Melbourne, Australia: Coopers & Lybrand (Australia).

Dane, F. C. (1990). *Research Methods*, Belmont, California: Wadsworth, Inc.

Fushimi, T. (1989). Corporate strategies and divisionalized management control at Matsushita, in *Japanese Management Accounting: A World Class Approach to Profit Management*, edited by Monden, Y. and Sakurai, M., Portland, Oregon: Productivity Press.

Hiramatsu, K. (1981). International accounting research in Japan: State-of-the-art, in *Multinational Accounting: A Research Framework for the Eighties*, edited by Choi, F. D. S., Ann Arbor, Michigan: UMI Research Press.

Itou, K. (2004). *Global Management Accounting*, Tokyo, Japan: Doubunkan-Shuppan (in Japanese).

Itou, Y. (ed.) (1995). *Globalization of Business Enterprises and Management Accounting*, Tokyo, Japan: Chuo-Keizai-Sha (in Japanese).

Kono, T. and Clegg, S. (2001). *Trends in Japanese Management: Continuing Strengths, Current Problems and Changing Priorities*, Hampshire, UK: Palgrave Publishers Ltd.

Kosuga, M. (1983). The trend of management accounting research in Japan: 1956–1982, *Kwansei Gakuin University Annual Studies* 32, pp. 153–166.

Kosuga, M. (1988). Relevance lost? State-of-the-art of management accounting research in Japan, *Kwansei Gakuin University Annual Studies* 37, pp. 135–146.

Kosuga, M. (1993). Current research issues in management accounting in Japan, *Kwansei Gakuin University Annual Studies* 42, pp. 75–89.

Kosuga, M. (2007). The relationship between strategies, organizational design, and management control systems at Matsushita, in *Japanese Management Accounting Today*, edited by Monden, Y. *et al.*, Singapore: World Scientific Publishing Co., Pte. Ltd., pp. 35–48.

Lawrence, P. and Lorsch, J. (1967). *Organization and Environment*, Boston, MA: Division of Research, Harvard Business School.

Matsushita Electric Industrial Co., Ltd. (2002). Annual Report.

Matsushita Electric Industrial Co., Ltd. (2003). Annual Report.

Matsushita Electric Industrial Co., Ltd. (2004). Annual Report.

Miyamoto, K. (1983). *Fundamentals of International Management Accounting*, Tokyo, Japan: Chuo-Keizai-Sha (in Japanese).

Miyamoto, K. (1989). *Management Accounting for Multinational Enterprises*, Tokyo, Japan: Chuo-Keizai-Sha (in Japanese).

Miyamoto, K. (2003). *Management Accounting in Global Enterprises*, Tokyo, Japan: Chuo-Keizai-Sha (in Japanese).

Miyamoto, K. and Kosuga, M. (2006). Management accounting in Japanese multi-national corporations: Lessons from Matsushita and SANYO, in *Value-Based Management of the Rising Sun*, edited by Monden, Y. *et al.*, Singapore: World Scientific Publishing Co., Pte. Ltd., pp. 181–195.

Miyamoto, K., Kosuga, M., Sakate, K., Asakura, Y., Ohara, A., Toyoda, T., and Kimura, A. (2005). International management accounting practices of Japanese enterprises in the electronics industry: A case study of Sharp Corporation, in *Management Accounting in Asia*, edited by Nishimura, A. and Willett, R., Singapore: Thomson Learning (a division of Thomson Asia Pte. Ltd.), pp. 189–204.

Monden, Y. (1985). Japanese management control systems, in *Innovations in Management: The Japanese Corporation*, edited by Monden, Y. *et al.*, Atlanta, Georgia: Industrial Engineering and Management Press.

Monden, Y. (ed.) (2000). *Japanese Cost Management*, London, UK: Imperial College Press.

Monden, Y. and Sakurai, M. (eds.) (1989). *Japanese Management Accounting: A World Class Approach to Profit Management*, Cambridge, Massachusetts: Productivity Press.

Nakagawa, M. (2004). *Globalization of Management Accounting*, Tokyo, Japan: Moriyama-Shoten (in Japanese).

Okano, H. (2003). *Global Strategy and Accounting*, Tokyo, Japan: Yuhikaku (in Japanese).

Okano, H. and Suzuki, T. (2007). A history of Japanese management accounting, in *Handbook of Management Accounting Research*, Vol. 2, edited by Chapman, C. S., Hopwood, A. G. and Shields, M. D., Oxford, UK: Elsevier Ltd., pp. 1119–1137.

Pascale, R. T. and Athos, A. G. (1982). *The Art of Japanese Management: Applications for American Executives*, London, UK: Penguin Books Ltd.

Sakurai, M. and Scabrough, D. P. (1995). *Integrated Cost Management*, Portland, Oregon: Productivity Press.

Sakurai, M. and Scabrough, D. P. (1997). *Japanese Cost Management*, Menlo Park, California: Crisp Publishing, Inc.

SANYO Electric Co., Ltd. (2003). Annual Report.

SANYO Electric Co., Ltd. (2004). Annual Report.

SANYO Electric Co., Ltd. (2005). Annual Report.

Ueno, S. (ed.) (2007). *Management Accounting Practices among Japanese MNEs: Finding from a Mail Questionnaire Survey*, Tokyo, Japan: Zeimu-Keiri-Kyoukai (in Japanese).

Yin, R. K. (1984). *Case Study Research: Design and Methods*, Newberry Park, California: Sage Publications.

Yoshida, H. and Shiba, K. (eds.) (1997). *Global Business and Accounting: Managerial, Financial and Governmental*, Tokyo, Japan: Zeimu-Keiri-Kyoukai (in Japanese).

Yoshikawa, T., Mitchell, F. and Moyes, J. (1994). *A Review of Japanese Management Accounting Literature and Bibliography*, London, UK: The Chartered Institute of Management Accountants.

Index

About the Volume Editor

Kanji Miyamoto
Professor of Faculty of Corporate Intelligence, Osaka Gakuin University, Osaka, Japan
Majoring in International Management Accounting
BA from Kwansei Gakuin University, MBA from Kwansei Gakuin University, MBA from Michigan State University, Ph.D. from Kwansei Gakuin University

Main Publications:
Fundamentals of International Managerial Accounting, Chuoukeizai-sha, Inc., 1983 (in Japanese).
Managerial Accounting in Multinational Enterprises, Chuoukeizai-sha, Inc., 1989 (in Japanese).
Managerial Accounting in Global Enterprises, Chuoukeizai-sha, Inc., 2003 (in Japanese).
Value-Based Management of the Rising Sun, World Scientific, 2006 (co-editor).